W9-DCU-442

WITHDRAWN FROM LIBRARY

The Politics of Income Inequality in the United States

This book revolves around one central question: Do political dynamics have a systematic and predictable influence on distributional outcomes in the United States? The answer is a resounding yes. Utilizing data from mass income surveys, elite surveys, and aggregate time series, as well as theoretical insights from both American and comparative politics, Kelly shows that income inequality is a fundamental part of the U.S. macro political system. Shifts in public opinion, party control of government, and the ideological direction of policy all have important consequences for distributional outcomes. Specifically, shifts to the left produce reductions in inequality through two mechanisms – explicit redistribution and market conditioning. Whereas many previous studies focus only on the distributional impact of redistribution, this book shows that such a narrow strategy is misguided. In fact, market mechanisms matter far more than traditional redistribution in translating macro political shifts into distributional outcomes.

Nathan J. Kelly is Assistant Professor of Political Science at the University of Tennessee. He received an M.A. and Ph.D. in political science from the University of North Carolina at Chapel Hill and a B.A. from Wheaton College (IL). He is the winner of the Raymond Dawson Fellowship and the James Prothro Award from the University of North Carolina Department of Political Science and was named a finalist for the E. E. Schattschneider Award for the best dissertation in American politics, awarded by the American Political Science Association. His research, supported in part by a grant from the National Science Foundation, has appeared in various journals, including *the American Journal of Political Science* and *Political Analysis*.

WITHDRAWN FROM LIBRARY

To Bud Kellstedt, for showing me how exciting the research
enterprise can be

and

To Jana, for never letting me forget that inequality exists, and
that it matters

MONTGOMERY COLLEGE
ROCKVILLE CAMPUS LIBRARY
ROCKVILLE, MARYLAND

The Politics of Income Inequality in the United States

NATHAN J. KELLY

University of Tennessee

CAMBRIDGE
UNIVERSITY PRESS

-146(223
FEB 1 4 2012

CAMBRIDGE UNIVERSITY PRESS
Cambridge, New York, Melbourne, Madrid, Cape Town, Singapore,
São Paulo, Delhi, Dubai, Tokyo, Mexico City

Cambridge University Press
32 Avenue of the Americas, New York, NY 10013-2473, USA

www.cambridge.org
Information on this title: www.cambridge.org/9781107400368

© Nathan J. Kelly 2008

This publication is in copyright. Subject to statutory exception
and to the provisions of relevant collective licensing agreements,
no reproduction of any part may take place without the written
permission of Cambridge University Press.

First published 2009
Reprinted 2009, 2010
First paperback edition 2011

A catalog record for this publication is available from the British Library.

Library of Congress Cataloging in Publication Data
Kelly, Nathan J.
  The politics of income inequality in the United States / Nathan J. Kelly.
    p.   cm.
  Includes bibliographical references and index.
  ISBN 978-0-521-51458-3 (hardback)
  1. Income distribution – United States. 2. Equality – United States.
  3. United States – Economic policy. I. Title.
  HC110.I5K45   2009
  339.2'20973–dc22   2008055111

ISBN 978-0-521-51458-3 Hardback
ISBN 978-1-107-40036-8 Paperback

Cambridge University Press has no responsibility for the persistence or accuracy of URLs for
external or third-party Internet Web sites referred to in this publication and does not guarantee
that any content on such Web sites is, or will remain, accurate or appropriate.

Contents

Figures

Tables

Acknowledgments

It is trite, but certainly true, that authors accrue several debts of gratitude in the course of any project. I am no exception. The initial idea for this book sprang from a conversation with Jim Stimson during graduate school. Jim's contributions to this effort did not stop with that initial conversation. For many months, he worked tirelessly to help me refine ideas and develop the skills necessary to test them. Along the way, the early stages of this research agenda led to a dissertation, which Jim directed. Simply stated, this project would not have come to fruition without the help and support of Jim Stimson.

I also appreciate the help that the other members of my dissertation committee – David Lowery, Mike MacKuen, George Rabinowitz, and John Stephens – provided in moving this project from a dissertation to a book. David Lowery was particularly helpful in pointing me in some useful directions at the beginning of the project, and John Stephens was the first to suggest that I explore how comparative theories might enhance my work.

During the course of this project, several people have read and commented on aspects of the research program. I thank the following people for their generosity and thoughtful consideration of my work: Michelle Benson, Johanna Birnir, David Brule, Ian Down, Sean Erlich, Chuck Finocchiaro, Richard Fording, David Houston, Mark Hurwitz, Wonjae Hwang, Gregg Johnson, Christine Kelleher, Paul Kellstedt, Jens Ludwig, Andrea McAtee, Jana Morgan, Tony Nownes, Mark Rom, Matt Schneider, Paul Senese, Terry Sullivan, Chris Wlezien,

Jennifer Wolak, the political science departments at the University at Buffalo and Tufts University, and participants in the Duke-UNC American Politics Research Group. I am also grateful to Chris Reinard and James Trimble for their research assistance and to Marcus Friesen for his invaluable help during my time in Washington, DC.

The political science departments at the University of Tennessee, the University at Buffalo, and the University of North Carolina supported this project though travel funding, administrative support, and release-time from teaching. Grants and awards funding this project came from the following organizations: the Duke-UNC American Politics Research Group, the Chancellor's Office at the University of Tennessee, and the National Science Foundation (Grant Number SES-0318044). Any opinions, findings, and conclusions or recommendations expressed in the material are, of course, mine and do not necessarily reflect the views of any of the funding organizations.

Eric Crahan has been a joy to work with. I thank him for his support of this project and his professionalism throughout the process. Also, every member of the staff at Cambridge has worked to make the publication process as smooth as possible. Small portions of Chapters 4 and 5 of this book are reprinted from an earlier article (Kelly 2005). I thank Blackwell Publishing and the Midwest Political Science Association for granting permission to reprint this material here.

The work to produce this book took many years, and there were numerous individuals in my life during this time who provided me with various forms of support and encouragement. I owe special thanks to the following dear friends: Doug Banister, Ashlea Catalana, Michael Catalana, Lynn Charles, Kathy Evans, Turner Howard, Jeremy Jennings, Mary Jennings, Breese Johnson, David Johnson, Peter Johnson, Travetta Johnson, Heather Kane, Patrick King, Judy Long, Kevin O'Donovan, Laurens Tullock, Polly Tullock, Ashley Walker, and Russ Walker. My parents, Connie Kelly and Milt Kelly, as well as my in-laws, Kathy Morgan and Harry Morgan, have been extraordinarily supportive. I also thank my brothers, Jon Kelly and Ben Kelly, as well as my siblings-in-law, Alyssa Lovell and Matt Lovell, for always pushing me to be my best.

Finally, I owe the largest debt of gratitude to Jana Morgan. Her support of this project has been both professional and personal. I first thank Jana for commenting on every component of this research program from start to finish. In fact, the earlier reference to John Stephens's help on this project would not have happened had Jana not pressed me to seek John as an addition to my dissertation committee. She has continually pushed my thinking in new and better directions. Jana also poured over every page of this manuscript. Her eye for detail prevented several errors, and, I am sure, made this book better in innumerable ways. Remaining errors, however, are mine alone. Jana is the best professional colleague that I could have asked for on this project.

Her support goes well beyond the professional. People ask me all the time what it is like to have a spouse who shares my profession. The premise always seems to be that it must be very hard. While it is true that our professional lives can pervade almost everything we do, my response to this common query is always the same – "It's great!" I consider myself one of the most fortunate people in the world to have a spouse who not only understands me but understands my work as well. Throughout this project, Jana always provided the sort of spousal encouragement that is typically acknowledged by authors. She prodded during times of discouragement or lack of energy. She provided reality checks when I (rarely) thought things were perfect. She gave me the freedom to do what I needed to do to see this project to completion. But on top of all this, Jana understands theory development, research design, and quantitative analysis. I am not sure what more I could ask!

1

Explaining Income Inequality

"Who gets what?" is arguably the most important question of political contestation. The answer to this question determines equality and inequality in society. Of course there are many forms of inequality. Political inequality, racial inequality, social inequality, power inequality, and economic inequality, to name a few, have received attention from journalists, pundits, and social commentators, as well as scholars from a variety of academic disciplines (Danziger and Gottschalk 1995, Harris et al. 2004, Johnston 2007, Keister 2000, McCarty et al. 2006, Page and Simmons 2000). While various forms of inequality are almost certainly interconnected, this book explicitly examines one specific form of inequality – economic inequality.

I focus on income distribution as a primary indicator of economic inequality.[1] The amount of inequality present in the income distribution presents an empirical answer to the question of "Who gets what?" I assess the (national) government role, the actions and policies by which government balances – or unbalances – the scales of equality.

---

[1] The other primary indicator of economic inequality that I considered analyzing is wealth inequality. I elected to focus on income inequality for three primary reasons. First, income is an important determinant of the material goods that people can obtain in the short term while wealth is a better indicator of long-term economic well-being, and politics more commonly focuses on the short term. Second, high-quality data on incomes in the United States are readily available over a long time-span, but wealth data are only available more recently and the data are of much lower quality. Finally, income inequality is the most commonly discussed distributional outcome in recent studies of U.S. politics.

Much of the story of equality and inequality must be a tale of changes in a market economy. But an important and often neglected part of the story concerns government and how policies benefit some people at the expense of others. That is my focus.

When Richard Nixon took the oath of office in 1969, he inherited an economy in which American incomes were more equal than when his predecessor took office, more equal in fact than ever before. While the most reliable data on income inequality go back only to the late 1940s, evidence pieced together by economic historians indicates that after a spike in inequality precipitated by the Great Depression, inequality declined steadily for several decades. Every four-year period brought a new level of equality to American society. It was never to be again. Following the Nixon/Ford presidencies, every new president took control of an economy that was less equal than it had been four years before. How could America trend toward equality for most of the twentieth century and then reverse course?

EQUALITY AND INEQUALITY IN THE WORLD'S RICHEST COUNTRY

Despite some recent and dramatic difficulties, there is no doubt that citizens of the United States participate in one of the most prosperous economies in the world. I begin exploring income inequality by providing a detailed look at who has the money in the United States. The goal is to paint a basic picture of economic conditions in the United States and describe how the economic pie is divided.

Economic Prosperity in the United States

How prosperous is the United States? There are several approaches to answering this question. One of them is to compare the United States to other countries around the globe. In Table 1.1, I report the U.S. ranking among OECD countries for several economic indicators. One of the most basic gauges of a country's aggregate prosperity is the total value of goods and services it produces within its borders. By this most rudimentary measure, in the year 2000 the United States was the largest economy in the world. With a GDP of nearly $10 trillion, the United

TABLE 1.1. *Aggregate Economic Indicators in the United States, 2000*

Indicator	OECD Rank out of 30
GDP	1 ($9,764 billion)
GDP Growth	6 (6%)
GDP Per Capita (Exchange Rate Method)	4 ($34,575)
Unemployment	5 (4%)
Inflation	9 (2%)

Source: OECD and World Bank.

States' nearest competitor was Japan, with an economy approximately half as large.

The overall size of an economy, however, could be only marginally related to the prosperity of its individual members. China, for example, has a large GDP, but its population is also large. But the United States is also near the top of the heap in GDP per capita and, in addition, has comparatively low rates of inflation and unemployment. In 2000, money and jobs were plentiful and prices were relatively stable. Though the situation has ebbed somewhat in the intervening period, this has been a common description of economic conditions for much of America's recent past.

If we look underneath these highly aggregated numbers, we find that the average American family at the end of the twentieth century clearly enjoyed the material fruits of a strong aggregate economy (see Table 1.2). The median price of a new home was $169,000, Americans owned 2.1 automobiles per household, and they spent more than $4000 annually per household on hotels and restaurants. With a median household income of more than $40,000 per year, the average American household was able to partake of a variety of goods and services that residents of many other countries would consider luxuries. When American households spend more than $100 per year on audio compact disks and more than $700 on alcoholic beverages, it would be hard to argue that the American macro economy is in crisis. While the U.S. economy goes through its ups and downs, Americans generally remain an economically privileged group. The United States undoubtedly has one of the most prosperous economies in the world.

TABLE 1.2. *Consumer Expenditures in the United States, 2000*

Measure	Value
Median Household Income	$41,578
Median Price of New Home	$169,000
% Households with Personal Computer	51%
% Households with Internet Connection	44%
Wireless Phone Subscribers Per Household	0.97
Telephone Lines Per Household	1.79
Automobiles per Household	2.1
Alcoholic Beverages Expenditures Per Household	$711
Tobacco Expenditures Per Household	$677
Hotel and Restaurant Expenditures Per Household	$4138
Compact Disk Expenditures Per Household	$129

Sources: U.S. Census Bureau; Euromonitor (2002).

Big and Small Slices of a Large Economic Pie

The economic pie in the United States is large, but the way it is divided is also important. When we start to talk about politics – who gets what – we are inherently focusing on areas of conflict, and politics is what this book is about. An examination of who gets what in a society points us toward indicators of *relative* rather than *absolute* prosperity. Income inequality is a key indicator of relative prosperity, and it is my focus.

Figure 1.1 presents a rudimentary picture of how economic prosperity is divvied up in the United States.[2] In this figure, I report the

---

[2] The data here and in the rest of the book come from the March Supplement to the Current Population Study (CPS) conducted by the United States Census Bureau. The CPS is a monthly survey of American households. Each month, approximately 50,000 households are sampled for participation in the CPS, and respondents are interviewed in order to obtain information about the employment status, earnings, hours of work, demographics, and educational attainment of all members of the sampled household over the age of 15. While this monthly survey collects information about wages earned by the various members of the household, it does not provide any more detailed information about the income earned within the household. However, on an annual basis, the CPS asks more detailed questions about income and work experience from the previous year in the Annual Demographic Survey, or March Supplement to the CPS. Beginning in 2003, the Annual Demographic Survey is called the Annual Social and Economic Supplement (ASES).

As far back as 1947, the CPS (it was the April survey in that time) asked respondents about the income from a handful of general sources earned during the previous year by members of the household. In the most recent data, information about income from over 50 separate sources including earnings, wages, tips, and government cash

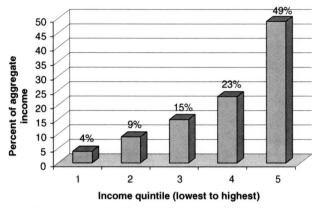

FIGURE 1.1. Share of Household Money Income Held by Each Quintile in the United States, 2000

share of aggregate *money* income held by each income quintile, from poorest to richest.[3] Later in the book I expand the examination beyond the basic money income definition that is the standard reported by the U.S. Census Bureau. This is a good place to start, though, because when the news reports that "median household income rose by 2.3 percent between 1986 and 1987," it refers to money income.[4]

What Figure 1.1 makes crystal clear is that the blessings of economic prosperity in the United States do not fall equally on everyone. Some

---

benefits is solicited. This makes the March CPS the most comprehensive, consistently available source of household income data in the United States.

[3] The household is the unit of analysis utilized throughout this book. One could also examine income inequality across families, or individuals, or even counties for that matter. The decision regarding unit of analysis is not trivial, and households are generally viewed as the most appropriate and inclusive unit of analysis. Analyzing only families, for example, excludes unrelated people living together in a housing unit. Examining individuals raises obvious problems about the inclusion or exclusion of children. Households include families and unrelated individuals and create fairly comparable units of analysis, though important differences across households will always exist.

[4] Money income can be thought of as income that comes or could come in the form of a direct cash payment. Specifically, money income includes the following sources: earnings from an employer, unemployment compensation, workers' compensation, Social Security, Supplemental Security Income, public assistance, veterans' payments, survivor benefits, disability benefits, pension or retirement income, interest, dividends, rents, royalties, estates, trusts, educational assistance, alimony, child support, financial assistance from outside the household, and other money income.

have a lot, while others have relatively little. Keep in mind that each income quintile represents exactly the same number of households. The top income quintile, however, received vastly more income than the households in the bottom quintile. In fact, the top 20 percent of households received about 3.25 times as much income as the bottom 40 percent combined, and the richest quintile was, in fact, more than 12 times richer than the poorest quintile of households.

A second way to view the division of the economic pie in the United States is to examine the household income levels at different positions in the income distribution. To make the concept of income inequality more readily grasped, I report the amount of money income received by households at specified points in the income distribution (see Table 1.3). How much income does the household at the 10th percentile (the household richer than 10 percent of other households) make compared to the household at the 95th percentile?

While it may be hard to understand the meaning of the fact that the bottom income quintile receives 4 percent of aggregate income, it should be easy to comprehend that the household at the 10th percentile of the U.S. income distribution earns an income of $10,991.

TABLE 1.3. *Income at Selected Positions in the Income Distribution,* 2000

Percentile	Income	Example Occupations
10th	$10,991	Food Preparation; Teachers' Aide
20th	$18,000	Nursery Worker; Dental Assistant; Security Guard; Bank Teller
30th	$25,030	Food Service Supervisor; Truck Driver; Machine Operators
40th	$32,763	Auto Mechanic; Dental Hygienist
50th	$41,990	Plumber; Technical Writer
60th	$51,565	Architect; Elementary Teacher
70th	$64,002	Financial Manager; Sales-Financial Services
80th	$80,288	Full Professor (Doctoral); Attorney
90th	$109,264	Advertising Executive
95th	$143,500	Family Practice Physician

Note: Listed example occupations approximate average annual income for full and part-time employees at the specified percentile.

Sources: U.S. Census Bureau, Bureau of Labor Statistics, American Association of University Professionals.

Essentially, the household richer than 10 percent of other households makes slightly more than $10,000 each year, including income from government benefit programs that provide cash assistance (like Social Security or welfare). It is probably difficult for many readers to imagine living on around $10,000 (graduate students toiling away as teaching assistants clearly excepted). About 10 percent of households in the United States, in fact, live on that much or less. At the other end of the spectrum, households at the 95th percentile make over $140,000 each year. It seems to be part of the current American mythology that none of us is "rich" or "poor." This is clearly not correct.

This table also lists occupations with wages approximating certain points in the income distribution. An average teachers' aide, for example, earns an annual income approximating the 10th percentile. An average family practice physician, on the other hand, would be at about the 90th to 95th income percentile (even after paying the high malpractice premiums we hear so much about). A full professor at a research university is, on average, richer than about 80 percent of the population.

It should be noted that the occupation listings provide only a rough picture. Many households have more than one income earner, and the occupations listed would put a single earner at the specified point in the income distribution. Imagine, for example, a household comprised of a plumber and a technical writer. This household would be at about the 80th percentile when the earnings are combined. Furthermore, some of the occupations listed at the bottom of the income distribution are there in large part because so many employees in these occupations work part-time. Employees who work less than 40 hours per week push the average annual earnings downward. It is still accurate to say, however, that an average person working in a field in which part-time work is prevalent earns less than an average person working in a field, with comparable hourly wages, in which part-time jobs are less prevalent.

American Inequality in Comparative Perspective

There is a substantial income gap between the richest and poorest Americans. The top 20 percent of households has more than 12 times

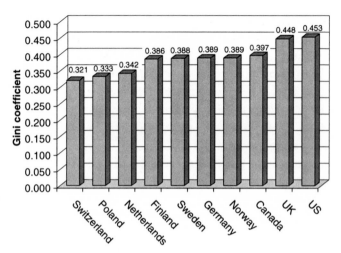

FIGURE I.2. Income Inequality in Nine Countries

as much income as the bottom 20 percent, and this is undeniably a large discrepancy in terms of absolute size. To this point, however, we have little in the way of context. How substantial is income inequality in the United States in relative terms? One way to gain some perspective on this question is to compare the United States to other countries.[5]

Figure 1.2 shows the Gini[6] coefficient of income inequality in ten countries for which comparable data were available in wave five of the Luxembourg Income Study (LIS) – Switzerland, Poland, the Netherlands, Finland, Sweden, Germany, Norway, Canada, the United Kingdom, and the United States. The data presented here show that the United States has higher levels of income inequality than other developed countries. While I focus here on just the countries available in the most recent LIS data, neither the specific countries available for analysis nor the measure of inequality used dramatically influences this result. Comparative studies of income inequality consistently show that inequality in the United States is among the highest of any developed

---

[5] Achieving data-comparability in cross-national examinations of income inequality is not easy. In fact, data-comparability problems limited scholarly comparative research on income inequality for decades. Recently, many comparability problems have been overcome, and the highest quality cross-national income data currently come from the LIS.

[6] The Gini ranges from zero to one with higher scores indicating more inequality.

democracy (Brandolini and Smeeding 2006, Gottschalk and Smeeding 1997, Pontusson and Kenworthy 2005). Both our rich and our poor are farther from the middle than in most other developed countries.

TRENDS IN U.S. INCOME INEQUALITY

Thus far we have seen a snapshot of income inequality at the dawn of the twenty-first century. If we wish to understand how political dynamics influence distributional outcomes, however, we must move beyond a cross-sectional snapshot. We need to examine how income inequality has changed over time. Explaining the substantial movement over time of inequality is the primary goal of the book.

To the degree that we can plumb it with the tools of economic history, it is clearly the case that much of the twentieth century was a time of major gains in income equality in the United States. Broken by the Great Depression, the trend until 1973 was toward more income *equality*. A surging industrial economy, the establishment of collective bargaining over wages, and the labor shortages of four wartime periods all helped to establish a society and economy in which the difference between extremes of affluence and poverty was moderate – small by historical standards.

Since 1973 (or some time in the early to mid-1970s) it is equally clear that the trend has reversed. For more than three decades now, most years in America have been less equal than the year before. Moderated by the ups and downs of the economy, the underlying trend is a march toward inequality. The America of the new third millennium is substantially more unequal than its predecessor societies. Perhaps more important, there is no indication in sight that the trend toward greater income inequality has broken. Absent remarkable changes in social and economic organization, it appears likely that the America of decades to come will be one of stark differentials, perhaps one of two societies with vastly divergent economic experiences.

In Figure 1.3, I use a series provided by economic historians (Plotnick et al. 2000) together with modern data on household incomes from the Census Bureau to plot the path of the Gini from 1913 to 2000. The Gini time series displays the pattern just described – a trend toward equality (i.e., smaller values of Gini) disrupted by the turmoil of the Great Depression and then continuing apace until the early 1970s. This

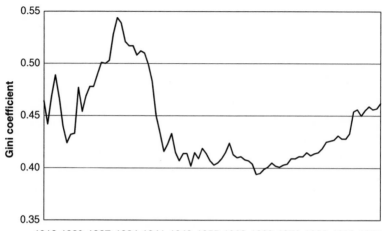

FIGURE 1.3. Gini Coefficient: 1913–2000

is followed by movement in the other direction, a growth of the Gini (and the inequality it represents) from 1973 through the end of the twentieth century.

To get a somewhat different view of the matter, I look simply at how much of the total national income is received by the upper 5 percent of citizens (Figure 1.4). This simple descriptive statistic tells essentially the same story. This highest income group received about a third of all income early in the century. That share steadily declined into the early 1970s to a level a little above 15 percent and then grew to about 22 percent by the century's end. Thus the experience of the richest Americans mirrors that of the whole distribution seen in the summary Gini coefficient. Here, as with the Gini, the arrow points toward a future in which Americans at the top will have an ever greater share of the total income relative to those at the bottom.

The early 1970s was clearly a turning point in the story of equality and inequality in America. So what happened? Who has been winning and losing since this crucial reversal? To answer this question I examine the experience of income classes over time.[7] Figure 1.5 shows how

---

[7] It is useful to remember that income classes are not really "classes" in the sense of impermeable boundaries. Not only do some people experience social mobility, but many people experience mobility associated with age and life position. Professors, for

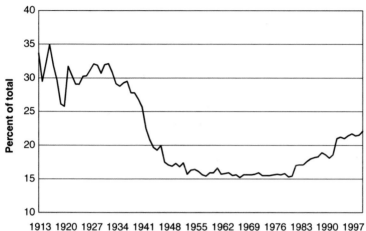

FIGURE 1.4. Income Share of Top 5 Percent: 1913–2000

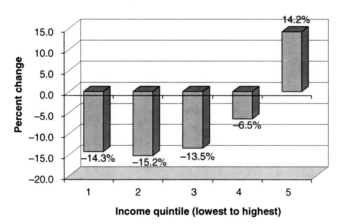

FIGURE 1.5. Changes in Income Share by Income Quintile: 1973–2000

the income share of each quintile changed between the beginning of
the inequality trend (1973) and 2000. Overall, the story is simple –
in relative terms, those at the top gained at the expense of everyone
else. The lowest income quintile began in 1973 with 4.2 percent of
aggregate income and ended in 2000 with just 3.6 percent – this is a

example, typically start their careers in quintiles 2 or 3 and complete them in the top
group.

14.3 percent decline. The story is similar for the bottom 80 percent – between 1973 and 2000, the bottom four quintiles all experienced a loss of income share. All of that loss was gained by the upper 20 percent, which began the era with 43.6 percent of aggregate income and ended with 49.8 percent – a 14.2 percent increase.

THEORETICAL FOUNDATIONS: POLITICAL DYNAMICS AND DISTRIBUTIONAL OUTCOMES

How can the path of income inequality in the last half of the twentieth century be explained? Efforts to answer this question have come from many disciplines, with some of the most commonly cited explanations of income inequality based on sociological and economic theory – the supply of or demand for skilled labor, business cycle fluctuations, technological change, single-female headed households, and rising female labor force participation. Political science has also contributed to this effort by examining the connection between social welfare programs and distributional outcomes (Hibbs and Dennis 1988, Page and Simmons 2000). But those attempting to synthesize the literature across disciplines have essentially concluded that the complex causal processes underlying the distribution of income are not well understood (Danziger and Gottschalk 1995, Jacobs and Skocpol 2005). Intellectually, this is not at all satisfying.

The goal of this book is to test an empirical model of distributional outcomes that explores the impact of aggregate level *political dynamics* in addition to sociological and economic explanations. Here at the outset, I describe this theoretical model in some detail so that it can be used as a reference through the remainder of the book. I draw on previous work in two areas – U.S. macro politics and comparative welfare states. Research in these traditions is related, but their development in different fields of political science has produced little cross-fertilization. By utilizing insights from both traditions, my work provides an important bridge between work done in American and comparative politics that leads to a fuller understanding of distributional processes.

From Mass Opinion to Societal Outcomes: The Macro Politics Model

The theoretical foundation of my research begins with the macro politics model of the U.S. governing system. The macro politics model examines relationships between parts of the U.S. governing system at the aggregate level such as public opinion, presidential approval, partisanship, elections, and public policy. The argument is that the parts of the system behave predictably and orderly. Citizens express preferences about competing policy alternatives, the preferred alternatives are enacted, and citizens then judge the quality of the outcomes produced. A growing set of results in the macro politics literature demonstrates systematic and understandable linkages between public opinion, elections, and policymaking. Liberal shifts in public opinion produce liberal shifts in policy because policymakers respond to changes in public opinion and, if they do not, are replaced through popular elections (Erikson et al. 2002, Page and Shapiro 1992, Stimson et al. 1995, Wlezien 1995). Simply stated, liberal public opinion leads to liberal policymaking both directly and through election outcomes. What we do not know is whether liberal policy making leads to expected outcomes, in the aggregate. In other words, does policymaking matter?

The fact that aggregate public opinion influences the course of public policy in the United States is an important underpinning of my model. But the macro politics model, in essence, assumes that the changes in public policy produced by election outcomes and mass preferences influence societal outcomes.[8] In the realm of income inequality, a leftward shift in policy should produce different distributional consequences than a move to the right according to the macro politics model. However, this implication has not been broadly tested.

If citizens exert influence over public policy but policy does not influence important societal outcomes, the substantive impact and the normative implications of the opinion-policy link decline. Figure 1.6 depicts the macro politics model with an extension to distributional outcomes. The connections between opinion, elections, and policy are fairly well-known. The connection between policy dynamics and distributional outcomes is not.

Studies too numerous to mention have examined the idea that government policies have distributional implications, but my approach makes a unique contribution. The effect on poverty and inequality of public education, health benefits, social insurance, public assistance programs, and taxes have been discussed time and again (Page and

---

[8] Though see Kellstedt et al. (1996) for evidence of policy's influence on racial equality.

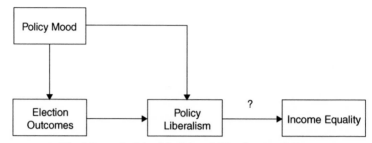

FIGURE 1.6. The Macro Politics Model and Distributional Outcomes

Simmons 2000, Pechman and Okner 1974, Pechman 1985). However, the existing discussion of public policy and distributional outcomes is largely based at the micro level (though one notable exception is provided by Kellstedt et al. (1996)). That is, the questions revolve around the impact of individual policies or policy domains. Rather than focusing only on the distributional impact of individual policies, I examine policy at the macro level – that is, collectively across issues and policy domains. While the micro perspective often sees policy enactments as the result of idiosyncratic forces specific to individual proposals, the macro perspective views policy as the systematic product of more general ideological and partisan conflicts that cut across issues. Given the centrality of distributional outcomes to political contestation, there should be a connection between macro policy and distributional outcomes.

Who gets what according to the macro politics model? According to this view, it is a consequence of aggregate political dynamics. The preferences of the mass public, who gets elected to office, and the policies enacted by policy makers should all play a role. This book provides an empirical assessment of whether this is the case.

Comparative Insights on American Inequality

Given that previous analyses of the macro politics model have not examined the distributional consequences of political dynamics, I turn to the welfare state literature to flesh out the mechanisms through which aggregate level political phenomena might influence distributional outcomes. The state-centric model (Skocpol and Amenta 1986), the logic of industrialism (Pampel and Williamson 1988, Wilensky

1975), and power resources theory (Esping-Andersen 1990, Huber et al. 1993, Huber and Stephens 2001, Korpi 1978, 1983, Stephens 1979) are the three leading theories of welfare state development. Each of these theories suggests different factors as influential in determining distributional outcomes. The state-centric model focuses on institutional structure and bureaucratic preferences, the logic of industrialism focuses on demographic and economic conditions, and power resources theory emphasizes the strength of lower class power resources in the form of left political parties and labor unions. Each of these theories informs the analysis in this book, but power resources theory has been cited as the dominant explanation of welfare state development in the extant comparative literature (Orloff 1996) and thus, is most central to my theoretical argument.

Power resources theory is rooted in the idea that the upper and lower classes have divergent distributional preferences, with the lower class favoring more egalitarian outcomes than the upper class. The theory goes on to argue that the lower classes must organize in order for their collective voice to be heard and influence outcomes. Power resources are the factors that facilitate organization, and the theory conceptualizes two realms in which the lower classes can organize – the economy and politics. Organization in the economic realm is evidenced by labor union strength, and organization in the political sphere is evidenced by the strength of left parties in government. Left-party control and union strength, in turn, influence distributional outcomes. Figure 1.7 depicts these connections.

The most important idea that I borrow from power resources theory is that distributional outcomes can be influenced *through the market and through the government*. Note in Figure 1.7 that market power

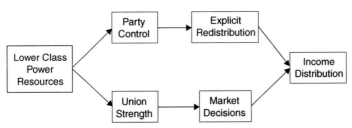

FIGURE 1.7. The Traditional Power Resources Model of Distributional Outcomes

resources evidenced by labor union strength produce an impact on market decisions and that political power resources evidenced by left parties influence state activity. Both state activity and market decisions, in turn, influence income inequality. As we will see in a moment, this idea becomes central in my overarching model of distributional outcomes in the United States.

A Combined Model of Distribution and Redistribution

The model of distributional outcomes analyzed in this book is presented in Figure 1.8. In part, this model is an explicit combination of the macro politics model and power resources theory. The chart demonstrates that there is a fundamental connection between these two theories. First, focus on the oval in the middle of the diagram. In the parlance of the macro politics model, "election outcomes" are discussed, while "party control of government" is utilized in the vernacular of power resources theory. These phrases express a similar concept, linking the two theories theoretically and empirically by a common component. Both theories are concerned with which political team controls the policymaking apparatus. Linking the two provides a comprehensive theoretical framework to analyze the macro political dynamics of income inequality in America.

This overarching model extends previous work in the macro politics and power resources traditions considered separately and provides

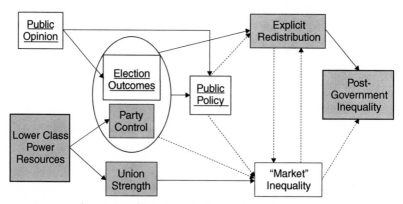

FIGURE 1.8. The Overarching Model: Combining Macro Politics and Power Resources

unique contributions to our general understanding of distributional processes. The shading of the boxes and the type of line connecting each component draw attention to the novel aspects of the model. The underlined text boxes show the key components of the macro politics model and the shaded text boxes represent components of power resources theory. The solid arrows between boxes show relationships that have been previously discovered, while the dashed arrows indicate connections that will be assessed for the first time in this book.

With reference to the U.S. macro politics literature, this model is in part a straightforward extension. Existing research generally does not examine the implications of policy shifts for societal outcomes. My model broadens this work through an explicit examination of the distributional implications of macro policy. Note here the lines connecting public policy to market inequality and redistribution. By implication, this extension of the macro politics model also provides for an assessment of popular influence over societal outcomes.

The theoretical extension of the macro politics model, however, goes beyond merely extending the analysis to assess whether policy affects the dynamics of inequality. I also examine how inequality reverberates back into the system. The figure contains arrows between market inequality and redistribution. Inequality and redistribution, as the key distributional outcomes analyzed in this book, are not just outcome variables, but also matter as a causal factor in their own right. The model posits that market inequality influences the choice of redistributional policies enacted and that the amount of redistribution achieved by government also affects market inequality. This places gains and losses in economic equality squarely within the *system* of American political dynamics, as both a consequence and a cause.

The contribution to power resources theory is a bit more nuanced. First, I add public policy as an explicit component of the power resources model. Previous research has not distinguished policymaking as a distinct causal stage. In existing work, party control leads directly to redistribution. Most proponents of power resources theory likely believe that party control is translated into societal outcomes via policy activity, but this has not been empirically examined in the comparative literature. Probably due in large part to a lack of comparable cross-national data, comparative research relies on observing

the connection between power resource variables and policy consequences like government redistribution, rather than directly observing
policy itself.[9] I bring public policy into the power resources model as
an indicator of power resources, with left policies indicating greater
lower class power resource mobilization.

The second extension of power resources theory is the connection
between power resources and market decisions. Following the lead of
Bradley et al. (2003), I conceptualize and measure the distributional
process in two stages. The first stage is driven primarily by private
market decisions. Firms decide how much to pay their employees,
individuals make investment decisions, and the price of commodities
fluctuates. All of these private decisions bear directly on the market
distribution of income. The second stage of the process is where government becomes explicitly involved by redistributing income – taking
money from some and giving it to others. Based on previous work in the
power resources literature, we would be forced to conclude that political dynamics matter only in the second stage – redistribution. Political
power resources (left parties) induce greater *redistribution*, and market power resources (labor unions) induce lower *market* inequality.
I add to power resources theory by exploring the possibility that political power resources influence not only redistribution but also market
inequality.

The impact of political power resources on market inequality would
occur via what I label a "market conditioning" mechanism. In general,
market conditioning refers to any situation in which private market
decisions that can be readily observed are influenced by government
action. Does government influence market decisions? This almost goes
without saying.

Large swaths of the tax code are designed for this very purpose.
Tax deductions for mortgage interest, charitable contributions, health
care, and business capital expenditures all influence private decisions.
The mortgage tax deduction provides a classic example. By virtue of
the fact that interest payments on home mortgages are deductible from

---

[9] Some comparative work appears to muddle the line between policy and outcomes by
using policy decisions such as social welfare expenditures as an indicator of redistribution. I define redistribution as impact rather than just effort, and policy as the
governmental decisions that are designed to influence society.

taxable income, home ownership is subsidized. At the margin, more homes are purchased because of this provision in the tax system. And in this case, those with high incomes tend to benefit the most.

Examples of market conditioning go far beyond tax expenditures. Job training programs provide skills to individuals that augment their employability. There are people currently employed who would not have been able to find jobs without previous experience in such training programs. Some people probably make investment decisions that they would not have made without government-required corporate reporting. Think also about how government construction of the interstate highway system has conditioned market outcomes. Railways became less prevalent, logistics companies began focusing on over the road applications, and businesses moved nearer to interstate hubs.

The common thread in all of these examples is that the market outcome we observe is different than it would be in a hypothetical world without government. Recent work in the American politics literature has begun to focus attention on government policies that condition market outcomes (Howard 1999, Page and Simmons 2000). It may even border on the tautological to say that government conditions market outcomes. That much is a given. Whether the market conditioning impact of government has implications for income inequality is another matter. I ask whether market conditioning has a systematic impact on the gap between rich and poor and whether this impact responds to macro political dynamics. If left parties and policies tip the scales of government conditioned market inequality in favor of the poor, this is evidence that market conditioning does influence income inequality systematically and in the direction predicted by power resources theory. Analyzing market conditioning as a potential mechanism for governmental influence on distributional outcomes represents a major theoretical advancement on current versions of power resources theory and the general literature on income inequality.

Who gets what? The central theme of the book is that government is an important determinant of the answer. I show that when the political landscape changes – a different party takes over the White House, the ideological direction of public policy shifts, or the mood of the public changes – income inequality responds in consistent and predictable ways. Shifts to the left produce more egalitarian outcomes and shifts to the right exacerbate existing inequality. Economic conditions matter for distributional outcomes, but I also demonstrate that political dynamics matter at least as much, and that the influence of politics manifests itself in some surprising ways. We expect government to influence distributional outcomes via explicit redistribution, but government also shapes income inequality by conditioning market outcomes. In fact, this mechanism of distributional impact is at least as strong as, and works in tandem with, redistribution.

AN OUTLINE OF THE BOOK

I pick up the story of government's role in equality and inequality in America in Chapter 2, where I introduce the theme of government's distributional impact. I discuss the policies that are most readily associated with income redistribution – tax and transfer programs. I compare the redistributional effect of programs such as Medicare, Social Security, unemployment benefits, and cash assistance policies. Then, I go on to discuss a second broad category of policies that can influence distributional outcomes via market conditioning. I argue that programs that do not explicitly redistribute income may be a particularly important part of the story in the United States.

The central message of Chapter 3 is that ideological and partisan disagreement over distributional outcomes is considerable in the United States. The first part of the chapter utilizes the debate over the marriage penalty tax in 2000 as a case study in distributional conflict. This tax policy provides a perfect example of political conflict over a policy with explicit distributional consequences, but one which was not broadly perceived as being primarily about income inequality. In the case study, I analyze the distributional differences between Republican and Democratic proposals, provide excerpts of floor debate addressing the distributional conflict, and draw on interviews I conducted with specific members of Congress. The second part of the chapter presents findings from a survey of members of Congress. I tentatively find that there are ideological and partisan disagreements in terms of the relative importance of distributional outcomes compared to other economic considerations. There are also differences regarding appropriate forms of government action to equalize both economic opportunity and outcomes.

Chapter 4 addresses one of the central questions of the book: Do national election outcomes influence distributional outcomes? I develop the overtime measures of inequality that will be central to the remainder of the analysis. I also discuss power resources theory in the context of the American case. I argue that convincing explanations of income inequality must account for politics in a systematic way. I then examine the effect of partisan control of the House, Senate, and presidency on redistribution and market income inequality from 1947 to 2000. I find that Democratic control of government not only influences explicit redistribution, but also influences market inequality.

The theme of assessing the connection between political dynamics and income inequality continues in Chapter 5, where I shift my focus from party dynamics to policy dynamics. This chapter is similar in organization to Chapter 4. I discuss why an examination of partisan control is only part of the picture and that an analysis of the policies produced by different partisan constellations of power is needed. I discuss the macro politics model in detail and show how my work extends existing research in an important direction – to an analysis of the substantive impact of policymaking. I find that shifts toward the left in public policy produce reductions in inequality. These reductions occur both because of more redistribution and because of reductions in inequality prior to taxes and transfers. I conclude based on this evidence that market conditioning as well as explicit redistribution are important political determinants of income inequality in America.

Chapter 6 links the analyses of the previous chapters together into a comprehensive analysis of income inequality in the United States. In the first part of this chapter, I answer the following questions: What is the total impact of politics on distributional outcomes? Is there a reciprocal linkage between redistribution and market inequality? Do mass preferences influence distributional outcomes? I find that the overall impact of politics rivals that of many economic factors and that market inequality and redistribution are interconnected. Redistribution drives market inequality higher, but lower market inequality drives redistribution down. I show that Democratic Party control of the White House and left policymaking reduce overall inequality, while surprisingly reducing explicit redistribution at the same time. I also demonstrate that public opinion has an important indirect influence on distributional outcomes via its influence on policymaking.

In Chapter 7, I discuss the future of income inequality in America and summarize the major findings of my research. I argue that the findings in this book, when coupled with what previous studies of the U.S. macro polity have taught us, show that political dynamics are central to distributional outcomes. More specifically, changes in mass attitudes produce changes in public policy through representational linkages. These changes in policy, in turn, substantively influence outcomes in the realm of income inequality. Thus, citizens can exert influence on an important contested outcome through democratic politics in the United States.

2

The Distributional Force of Government

Now as much as ever, government is pervasive. Regardless of values like liberty and freedom and limited government, the state influences numerous aspects of life. In nearly every recent national election campaign, we have seen candidates propose divergent policies on topics ranging from coal-fired power plants, to fuel efficiency standards, to national carbon emission targets, to provision of health insurance, to family planning policies, to educational goals, to free trade, and to employment policy. Government enacts policies ranging from the social sphere, to the economic sphere, to the environment, and so on. But what difference do government policies make for distributional outcomes?

In this chapter I focus on two major questions. First, what government activities have the potential for influencing income inequality? Second, how much impact do these policies have? Specifically, I discuss two broad mechanisms through which government can influence the distribution of income: explicit redistribution and market conditioning. I also discuss a straightforward strategy for measuring the influence of redistribution. Using income data from 2000, I examine the distributional effects of a wide variety of redistributional programs.

MECHANISMS OF DISTRIBUTIONAL IMPACT

There are any number of policies and programs that could be used to influence distributional outcomes. Many programs are clearly and closely tied to efforts to balance the scales between rich and poor. But these sorts of programs comprise only a portion of government activities in the United States. Politicians from both sides of the aisle are reticent to speak of redistribution – at least not with a positive tone. But if the question of "Who gets what?" is central to politics, there is likely more to the distributional impact of government than just policies explicitly aimed at balancing the scales of inequality.

Explicit Redistribution

When people think about programs that influence income inequality, the programs most likely to come to mind are explicitly redistributive – programs that take money from some (in the form of taxes) and give to others (in the form of benefit payments). Even the relatively small traditional welfare state operated in the United States includes a variety of redistributive programs, ranging from welfare to Social Security. The focus here is government policies that explicitly redistribute income from the top of the income distribution toward the bottom. What we want to know is the degree to which explicit government redistribution equalizes incomes in the United States.

The redistributive effect of a government program is straightforward in concept. It is the difference between the hypothetical income inequality that would exist in the absence of government activity and the income inequality that exists after government has acted. The empirical observation of this concept is, however, quite difficult. While income inequality as it has existed in the United States for the past several decades can be observed, a world in which government has not played a role simply does not exist. Thus, the full implications of government action on income distribution can be only imperfectly observed.

Many federal government programs influence the distribution of income. Some have effects that are hard to pinpoint. Other programs affect the distribution of income through either cash or in-kind benefits, and these are the kinds of programs I look at in this section. Food stamps, Social Security, Medicare, and a variety of other benefits fall under this category. But expenditures are only one side of the coin. Taxes have distributional consequences as well. While it is difficult or impossible to observe the *full* distributional effects of explicitly redistributive programs, available data can be used to measure the *direct* effects of government taxation and explicit benefits.

Consider the effects of Medicare in order to illustrate the idea of direct, first-order effects of a program as opposed to indirect, higher-order effects that are extremely difficult if not impossible to observe. The direct beneficiaries of Medicare are the elderly who seek medical care. It is simple enough to calculate the distributional impact of Medicare for these beneficiaries. Calculate household income excluding the value of Medicare benefits and compute inequality based on this income concept. Then calculate income including the value of Medicare benefits and measure the degree of inequality. The *first-order* effect of Medicare on inequality is the difference between pre-Medicare income inequality and post-Medicare income inequality. But how would the income of doctors be changed if Medicare did not exist? This is a question that cannot be answered empirically because we do not and cannot know (without myriad assumptions) what a physician's income would be in the absence of Medicare. It could be lower because some elderly might skip medical care without Medicare, but it could also be higher if doctors did not fill parts of their schedule with Medicare patients who, via government reimbursement to the physician, pay below-market rates for many procedures. Similar issues arise with welfare programs that may dissuade work effort at the same time that they provide cash to beneficiaries. It is difficult to know with precision exactly how much work is reduced by the receipt of benefits. When calculating distributional impact, then, I focus on what *can* be known – the direct, first-order impact of government programs.

In order to calculate the explicit distributional effect of a government program, the distribution of income excluding the program must be compared to the distribution of income including the program. The first step in calculating the distributional consequences of government programs is to define a baseline income distribution as a consistent point of comparison. This distribution should include only income that comes from market (nongovernmental) sources. Fortunately, with individual-level March CPS data, this task is straightforward.

In the previous chapter the focus was on household money income inequality. But money income, as an income concept, includes income from only a handful of government programs like public assistance that distribute benefits in the form of cash payments. This excludes in-kind benefits, like Medicare. So money income is not a sufficient income concept for the purpose of determining the distributional impact of individual government programs. As a baseline for comparison, I will focus on income excluding money from any government mandated, funded, or administered program. I call this concept pre-redistribution income, and it includes income from the following sources: earnings from an employer, employer health care contributions, capital gains, pension or retirement income, interest, dividends, rents, royalties, estates, trusts, alimony, child support, financial assistance from outside the household, and other money income that is not otherwise categorized.[1] Figure 2.1 shows the aggregate share of pre-redistribution income for each income quintile in the year 2000.

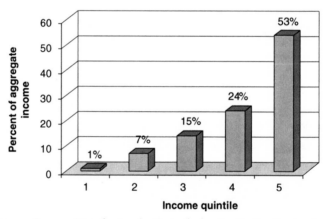

FIGURE 2.1. Income Distribution by Quintile for Pre-Redistribution Income

---

[1] One could argue that other governmental sources of income should also be excluded. For example, federal employees obviously receive their wages from the government. I view this type of government income source differently than government sources that provide payments (or mandate employer payments) for something other than labor. There are certainly some gray areas in this categorization. For example, workers' compensation income is not included in pre-redistribution income. Workers' compensation is paid jointly by the government and the injured worker's employer. Because it is a government mandated program that is at least partially funded out of government coffers, I exclude it from pre-redistribution income. On the other hand, child support payments are also, in a sense, mandated by government. However, these payments come completely from private funds and are thus included in pre-redistribution income.

We see in this figure that, prior to any explicit redistribution by government, the top income quintile held more income in 2000 than the bottom 80 percent of households combined. Measuring inequality excluding government benefits is the first step toward assessing the distributional consequences of government programs, and inequality in pre-redistribution income provides a baseline for assessing the distributional consequences of government programs in the United States. The second step is to determine how the distribution of income changes when benefits from a particular government program are reintroduced to the definition of income. In the sections that follow, I examine how taxation and benefit programs influenced income inequality in the United States during the year 2000.

The Distributional Impact of Taxation

There is no shortage of political debate and rhetoric about the federal government's system of taxation. On the one hand, Republicans almost always have some proposal in the works to flatten taxes so that everyone pays their "fair share," which in the eyes of many conservatives means all paying the same proportion of their income in taxes. Democrats, on the other hand, often bemoan the lack of fairness in the U.S. tax code that allows wealthy individuals to dodge taxes. The liberal viewpoint is that the tax system is weighted too far in favor of the rich. But what is the real story?

The national government in the United States collects several forms of taxes.[2] In terms of those that directly influence the amount of income taken home by U.S. households, these forms of taxation fall principally into two categories – income taxes and payroll taxes. Income taxes, as all of us in America are acutely aware, are based on the amount of income earned within a household. As one earns more money, the amount of taxes due on each additional dollar earned increases. The federal income tax, then, is in theory a progressive tax that takes greater percentages from those who earn large sums of money than from those

---

[2] My focus here is almost entirely on taxes collected by the national government. State and local governments also collect a variety of taxes, and some taxes collected at the state level are notoriously regressive, such as the sales tax. My analysis here does not account for taxes at all levels of government, but others have conducted detailed analyses of state and local taxation (Peppard and Roberts 1977).

who earn little. Of course the federal income tax is much more complicated than a simple increasing marginal tax rate. Tax liability is
reduced for those with expenditures on items ranging from higher education to home mortgage interest to hybrid gas/electric vehicles. All of
these deductions reduce taxable income, thereby reducing taxes paid.
Most deductions, in fact, are likely to benefit middle and upper income
households (like the mortgage interest deduction). Other programs that
are part of the federal income tax system are explicitly designed to help
the working poor (like the Earned Income Credit).[3]

Payroll taxes are somewhat different than income taxes. Payroll
taxes, as the name implies, are taxes collected based on how much
an employer pays each employee. The major federal payroll taxes are
Social Security, Medicare, and unemployment insurance. Payroll taxes
are determined as a percentage of wages paid to an employee, but part
of the tax is paid by the employee and part is paid by the employer. Furthermore, for both Social Security and unemployment, taxes are paid
only until the employee earns a specified amount. In 2000, for example, employees were required to pay 6.2 percent of the first $76,000
of their wages in Social Security tax, with a matching amount paid
by employers; amounts above that are not taxed. Medicare taxes are
apportioned via a flat rate that is shared by the employer and employee
with no earnings ceiling for the tax. Finally, unemployment taxes are
fully paid by the employer.

It should be fairly obvious that a tax structured like Social Security
will be regressive, taking a greater percentage of earnings from workers
with little income than from those high in the income distribution. Two
earners making $76,000 and $7,600,000, for example, pay identical
dollar amounts of Social Security taxes. I am interested primarily in
the direct effects of payroll taxes paid by the employee. Of course, at
least a part of the employer's portion of payroll taxes can be shifted

---

[3] Revenue lost by the federal government because of available deductions and programs
like the Earned Income Credit (EIC) are called tax expenditures. Tax expenditures are
a common way for government to give benefits to certain groups without having a fiscal
expenditure in terms of the government balance sheet. I treat tax expenditures as a part
of the tax system, but these government benefits are no different than others in the sense
that they can help some groups more than others, thereby influencing the distribution
of income. However, I do not conduct detailed analyses of the distributional effects
of individual tax expenditures, though others have (Howard 1999).

TABLE 2.1. *Distribution of Federal Taxes and Earned Income Credit,*
2000

Type of Tax	Pre-Redistribution Quintile (%)				
	1	2	3	4	5
Federal Income	0	3	8	18	71
Federal Payroll	1	8	17	26	48
Earned Income Credit	15	61	15	6	2
Total Federal Taxes	0	3	11	21	65
Share of Pre-Redistribution Income	1	7	15	24	53

to the employee in the form of reduced wages. However, I view this as an indirect effect of the tax program that varies by employer. In fact, most economists studying this issue find that employer payroll taxes are only partially shifted to employees (Beach and Balfour 1983, Holmlund 1983, Vroman 1974, Weitenberg 1969).

In Table 2.1, I begin to explore the distributional effects of several tax programs. This table shows the proportion of federal income and payroll taxes paid and Earned Income Credit (EIC) received by each pre-redistribution income quintile. A completely proportional tax (or credit) would be allocated between the income quintiles in the same proportion as pre-redistribution income. Not surprisingly, the first row of the table shows that federal income taxes are progressive. While the top income quintile has 53 percent of all pre-redistribution income, households in this quintile pay 71 percent of federal income taxes. The opposite is true for the first four quintiles.

We see in the second row that federal payroll taxes are regressive not only in design but in distributional impact. The bottom four income quintiles pay a larger proportion of their income in payroll taxes than does the top quintile. The most prominent part of the tax system that is designed to equalize incomes through aid to low and middle class working families (the Earned Income) clearly distributes benefits in a manner consistent with this goal. More than three-quarters of Earned Income benefits go to the bottom two income quintiles.[4] If we look

---

[4] On its face it is difficult to understand how less than 100 percent of Earned Income benefits go to the lowest income quintile. The income cutoffs for Earned Income eligibility for families with children, however, go well into the second quintile. In

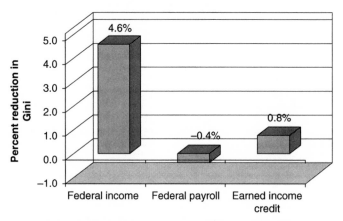

FIGURE 2.2. Reduction in Inequality Attributable to Federal Tax Programs in the United States

at the final two rows of the table, it is clear that the federal tax system appears to be at least moderately progressive – taking a greater percentage of income from the rich than from the poor. This is especially noticeable at the top of the income distribution, where the top quintile pays 65 percent of all federal taxes but holds 53 percent of all income.

The tangible effect of federal taxes on income inequality during the year 2000 is examined in Figure 2.2. This chart shows the percent reduction in the Gini coefficient that can be attributed to the forms of taxation discussed above. The federal tax program that has the single largest effect on income inequality is the federal income tax, which reduced income inequality from its pre-redistribution level by 4.6 percent during 2000.[5] The Earned Income Credit also equalizes incomes, but by a much smaller amount – less than 1 percent. Federal payroll

addition, even a few households in the higher quintiles can receive benefits due to differences between households and tax units. People in the same household (an adult child and parent, for example) can be taxed separately. Thus, a child of a high-income parent may qualify for the Earned Income despite the fact that household income is in the upper part of the distribution.

[5] This calculation, of course, does not include reductions in work effort, since it is calculated simply by computing inequality in income with taxes included as income and then again after subtracting taxes from income. Those at the top might have earned more pre-tax income were it not for the deterrent effects of a progressive marginal tax rate.

taxes, on the other hand, slightly increase inequality in the United States, and this result is driven primarily by the Social Security tax.[6]

The Distributional Impact of Government Expenditures

Federal taxes have some impact on the distribution of income, but the programs with the most readily apparent distributional consequences involve government expenditures. The programs that many Americans would probably name if asked which government programs give the most help to the poor would be means-tested programs – benefits like food stamps and welfare. These programs are specifically targeted toward the needy because an individual must be below a certain income level before attaining eligibility for the program. But means-tested programs make up a relatively small part of the national budget, much less than 5 percent, in fact. I begin my discussion of the distributional impact of expenditures with two large non-means-tested programs that are designed to ease the financial burden of the retired – Social Security and Medicare.

Social Security and Medicare

In some of the political commentary of the last two or three decades the twin retirement security programs, Social Security and Medicare, have been pictured as boondoggles for the newly affluent "senior" class. Designed as unabashed income redistribution schemes by Franklin Roosevelt and Lyndon Johnson, the two programs have ballooned dramatically as the numbers of retiree recipients have grown with an ever-increasing American life-span and will likely grow further as baby boomers enter retirement. It is commonly suggested that the programs have become entitlements for a politically influential group which, though it no longer needs the benefits, has life-and-death control over the policymakers who decide what to do. One can imagine a portrait along the lines of Ronald Reagan's famous "welfare queens," the

---

[6] More comprehensive tax incidence studies that examine state, local, and federal taxes that are not levied on individuals (like taxes on business profits) argue that the overall distributional effect of taxation in the United States is very minimal (Pechman 1985, Pechman and Okner 1974). The distribution of the tax burden is essentially proportional except for the richest and poorest households.

silver-haired retiree driving his Mercedes Benz to the country club, stopping off to deposit the monthly Social Security check.

Reality, however, is quite contrary to this image. The data on Social Security and Medicare recipients presented in Figures 2.3 and 2.4 tell the real story. Recipients are, for the most part, still the poorest Americans. And the income from these programs is for most of these people virtually all the income they have. Fifty-three percent of total Social Security benefits go to those in the lowest pre-redistribution income quintile, and only 23 percent of these benefits go to the top three quintiles combined. The distribution of Medicare benefits is similar, though not quite as skewed as Social Security.[7] The bottom 40 percent of households receive 66 percent of these benefits, and the top two quintiles garner only 19 percent. Clearly, Social Security and Medicare

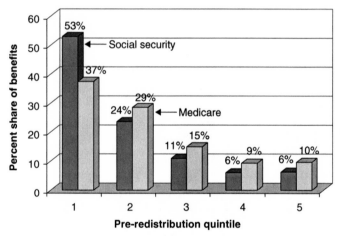

FIGURE 2.3. Share of Social Security and Medicare Benefits Received by Each Income Quintile

[7] Medicare is a noncash benefit that provides those over 65 with access to medical care. Since this benefit is not in the form of cash, there is some question about how to convert the benefits received into income. The March CPS values Medicare benefits using the fungible conversion method. Rather than converting Medicare benefits to income by computing the market value of the health care received, the fungible method determines the amount of money the household would have actually spent on health care had the benefit not been received. The assumption of this method is that households would have forgone health insurance if given the choice between food and insurance. So, the fungible method provides a conservative method for determining the redistributive effect of Medicare.

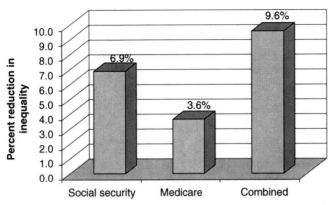

FIGURE 2.4. Reduction in Inequality Attributed to Social Security and Medicare Benefits

cannot be fairly characterized as a boon for the wealthy. In fact, this draws attention to the reason why many people in America are poor – they are old and can no longer work. To be perfectly clear, much of the bottom quintile is composed of individuals over age 65 who are retired. These are the primary recipients of the largest government benefit programs.

The equalizing effects of Social Security and Medicare are quite dramatic, so much as to dwarf all other federal programs. If the level of inequality after Social Security and Medicare (each treated separately) are compared to pre-redistribution inequality, we see that Social Security benefits reduce inequality by nearly 7 percent and Medicare reduces inequality by 3.6 percent (see Figure 2.4). When the effect of both programs is combined, the Gini coefficient drops from 0.52 to 0.47, a reduction of almost 10 percent. Examining just these two programs clearly shows that the greatest redistributive impact of government in the United States comes through expenditures rather than revenue collection. Without these two programs, nearly one-fifth of all Americans would essentially have no income.[8] These individuals would lack

---

[8] Some of these individuals would elect to continue working, but at some point this would obviously become impossible. Furthermore, it is hard to imagine that many people who subsist on Social Security and Medicare alone would not seek other forms of income under the current plan if they could. These benefits do not exactly provide for kingly living, but do allow elderly Americans to subsist during their retirement years.

income for food and housing and would then incur medical expenses (often associated with aging). However, they would not be able to pay for these expenses nor could they afford insurance to replace Medicare. This is not the welfare state that is the centerpiece of political dialogue. In dollar terms, however, it is the welfare state that matters. Everything else – particularly income assistance programs targeted toward the poor and the unemployed – is at the periphery. I turn now to describing the effects of those "other" programs.

Other Programs

The programs discussed in this section are an interesting combination of federal, state, and local activities, so isolating the effect of the national government in these programs is impossible. For example, Medicaid (the medical program for the poor) was initiated by the federal government, but is administered and partially funded by the states. States get to decide specific eligibility criteria and benefit levels, with funding shared by the national government. Some states would, no doubt, have similar programs without funding from the national government, but it is likely that funding levels would be lower and many states would forgo such programs completely. Strictly speaking, the effects of programs like Medicaid should be allocated between the state and national governments. However, I do not have any basis on which to make such an allocation with the data I am using. Therefore, I attribute the distributional effects of these programs to the federal government alone.

It would be desirable to array the redistributive effect (percent decrease in Gini attributable to income from each program) of all spending programs on a single graph such as Figure 2.4. But Social Security and Medicare had to be treated separately because their scale is so great that other programs look trivial in contrast. The programs are not trivial, and we can see in Figures 2.5 and 2.6 that some matter more than others.

Figure 2.5 shows the reduction in inequality that *non means-tested benefit programs* have in the United States. These are programs that have no income requirement for eligibility. In order to receive benefits from these programs, one has to be in a specified category of individuals, with these categories not being defined by income. To receive veterans' benefits, one must have fought in a foreign conflict for the

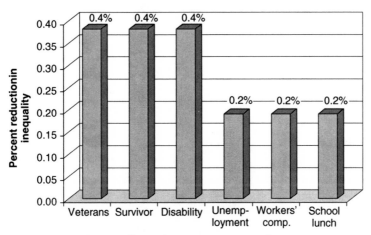

FIGURE 2.5. Equalizing Effect of Non-Means-Tested Government Benefit Programs

U.S. military. To receive school lunches, a household must have children attending a school that participates in the school lunch subsidy program.[9] The distributional impact of veterans', survivor, and disability benefits are similar, with each program reducing inequality by approximately 0.4 percent. Unemployment benefits, workers' compensation, and the school lunch program have an even smaller effect, reducing inequality by about 0.2 percent each.

Still, all of the programs discussed to this point are not what most Americans probably think of as the American welfare state. Rather, welfare is for those who are truly needy – the poorest in society. Programs that are targeted to the poor are *means-tested*. That is, receipt of the benefit is only for those below a certain income level. The income data collected by the Census Bureau includes benefits received in the following categories: Supplemental Security Income (SSI), public assistance, Medicaid, educational assistance, housing subsidies, and food stamps. The theme that ties all these programs together is that income below a certain threshold is a qualification necessary to receive the

---

[9] All children eating school-provided lunches benefit directly from the school lunch program. Children from poor households get additional benefits in the form of further reduced prices or free lunches. Other non means-tested programs have certain components that are means-tested, but the general benefit is not based on income. I categorize these programs as non-means-tested.

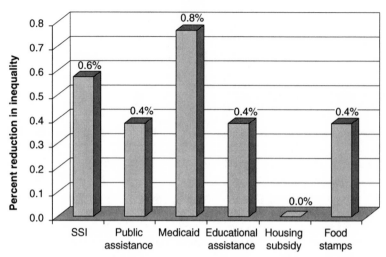

FIGURE 2.6. Equalizing Effect of Means-Tested Government Benefit Programs

benefit. Only those below a certain income threshold (determined by administering state agencies) can receive health care through Medicaid. The same is true for all means-tested programs.

The equalizing effects of these means-tested benefits are charted in Figure 2.6. This chart shows how much the Gini coefficient is reduced when benefits from each program are included in income as opposed to excluded from income. Of means-tested benefits, the largest equalizing effect is produced by Medicaid, but its 0.8 percent reduction in inequality is still small in comparison to the effects of Social Security and Medicare. The next largest effect is that of the SSI program. The public assistance programs that are so often at the center of political dialogue come next (public assistance and food stamps), but are only about half as large as Medicaid in their impact.

The Total Government Contribution to Equality in 2000

Now we have seen the distributional consequences of several individual government programs, from the income tax to welfare assistance. When the distribution of income excluding all government income sources is compared to the distribution including these sources one at a time, it becomes clear that nearly all government programs that

TABLE 2.2. *Distribution and Level of Income by Deciles in the United States, 2000*

Deciles	Pre-Redistribution Income		Post Government Income	
	Share (%)	Mean	Share (%)	Mean
1	0	$0	2	$10,988
2	1	$5,323	3	$16,835
3	3	$15,225	4	$22,182
4	4	$24,798	6	$28,226
5	6	$34,483	7	$34,281
6	8	$45,363	8	$42,339
7	10	$58,076	10	$51,982
8	13	$73,790	13	$63,710
9	18	$96,995	16	$80,460
10	36	$200,605	31	$156,855

explicitly take or give money to individuals equalize incomes.[10] The issue I turn to in this section is the tangible effect of government programs considered collectively.

I begin by comparing the distribution of income by deciles in Table 2.2. I use deciles in this case because they yield some insights that could not be seen in income shares by quintile. The first two columns show the income shares and levels of each income decile based on the now familiar concept of pre-redistribution income. The columns on the right of the table show the same information for a different income concept – post-government income. Post-government income accounts for the effects of taxes and government benefit programs by subtracting federal taxes from and adding the value of government benefits to pre-redistribution income.

The data in this table tell an interesting story. First of all, without government benefits, the bottom 10 percent of households would have essentially no income. These households consist primarily of elderly

---

[10] It is certainly not the case that every government policy, even redistributive policy, benefits the poor. There are some high-income individuals who receive Social Security benefits. Subsidies to higher education often directly benefit middle and upper income individuals more than the poor. Certain tax programs undoubtedly benefit the rich more than the poor (Johnston 2007). Despite this, to the extent that the impact of government programs can be measured with income data, the overall impact of government provides more benefits to the less well-off than the richest Americans.

individuals who do not work and have no private pension or retirement income. Without the government these individuals would have
no money for food, shelter, or basic health care. The second decile is
not much better off, with only a 1 percent share of aggregate income
and an average of a little over $5,000 available for basic expenses.
Those in the third and fourth income deciles have an average of over
$15,000 from nongovernment income sources – enough to provide a
basic standard of living in the United States, but by no means a luxu-
rious existence. At the other end of the income distribution, however,
households are very well-to-do prior to government action. The top
10 percent of households garnered approximately 36 percent of pre-
redistribution income in 2000, providing an average household income
of over $200,000.

The distribution of post-government income is quite different. The
two right columns of Table 2.2 show that households at the bottom
of the income distribution, while not getting rich by any means, are
more likely able to subsist on government benefits. The bottom decile
(of primarily retired persons) garnered a 2 percent share of aggregate
post-government income, with an average income of nearly $11,000.
The top of the income distribution is also substantially different, with
the income share of the top 10 percent reduced from 36 to 31 percent
by government programs and the average income of these households
reduced by a striking $44,000. This table also makes clear that the
lion's share of redistribution is from the top 20 percent of households
to the bottom 40 percent. The income share of the middle 40 percent
of households remains essentially the same between pre-redistribution
and post-government income.

Figure 2.7 quantifies the reduction in inequality that is caused by
certain types of government programs – taxes, mean-tested benefits,
non-means-tested benefits (both including and excluding Social Security and Medicare), all benefits combined, and the total effect of federal
taxes and benefits. This chart depicts an American welfare state that
is different from the one that is so often mythologized in political
debate. While distributional concerns are not often discussed openly
in American politics, they are most common in debates over taxes
and means-tested benefit programs. Democrats and Republicans have
pretty clear differences, for example, on how the tax burden should
be distributed, with those on the left continually pushing for more

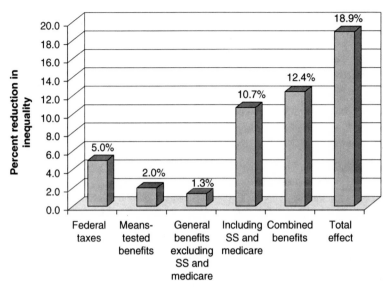

FIGURE 2.7. Combined Equalizing Effect of Government Action in the United States, 2000

progressive forms of taxation. What we see in this chart, however, is that taxes and means-tested benefits are not where the majority of redistributive action is. Taxes and means-tested programs do have an impact on income inequality, but taxes reduce inequality by only 5 percent, and means-tested programs equalize incomes by only 2 percent. This result probably should not be surprising. It would be difficult for programs that take up such a small portion of federal expenditures to make a massive difference in income inequality.

The more surprising result is for the effect of general benefit programs that are not specifically designed in such a way as to target the poor. Income inequality is not usually mentioned explicitly in political debate about these general benefit programs. Sometimes there are questions about whether benefits like Social Security and Medicare should be made at least somewhat contingent on income, and questions about the level of benefits that should be provided in these programs are also common. It is clear, however, that most of government's influence on income inequality is achieved through such programs. Non-means-tested benefits (excluding Social Security and Medicare) reduce income inequality by only 1.3 percent, but Social Security and Medicare have truly massive effects. When these two benefit programs are added, non-means-tested programs reduce inequality by a staggering 10.7 percent. In fact, more than 60 percent of government's 18.9 percent reduction in inequality through taxes and expenditures can be attributed to benefit programs that are not specifically targeted to the poor.

It is interesting that perhaps the two most popular benefit programs in the United States (Social Security and Medicare) are also the two most redistributive. Take away the progressive income tax, welfare of all kinds, unemployment compensation, disability, and on and on, and you produce effects on the income structure of Americans smaller than those produced by these two programs alone. For those on the political left who are frustrated by the degree of conservative sentiment in the United States, this information might be encouraging. Despite a general lack of concern about equalizing economic outcomes, two of the most sacred and untouchable programs in the United States are, in fact, highly redistributive. This phenomenon is actually not unique to the United States. In other more generous welfare states, many benefits are not so highly contingent on income. Welfare state generosity is politically feasible when government benefit programs are not about rich versus poor, but when the programs are designed to extend useful benefits to all citizens in society.

Given this, the two issues on the current American agenda that could have the largest distributional impact in the future are health care and Social Security. Making health care a guaranteed benefit would likely have an equalizing effect – perhaps a large one. Contrarily, minimizing or eliminating guaranteed benefits through Social Security would certainly have the opposite effect.

Market Conditioning

The programs that I have discussed to this point are probably the ones that come to mind most often when thinking about the distributional influence of government. Redistributional programs – those that explicitly take money from some through taxes and give to others via benefit programs – have clear and obvious distributional effects. Entitlement programs like Social Security and Medicare have the largest equalizing influence, but even when all explicitly redistributional programs are taken together, they do not begin to account for all government activity. I argue here that many, if not most, other government activities have the potential to influence distributional outcomes as well. Programs that are not explicitly redistributive can nonetheless influence distributional outcomes via a mechanism I call market conditioning.

Market conditioning arises when government action produces economic outcomes different than those which would be produced by market forces in the absence of government action – that is, when the state modifies or manipulates private market decisions. This is a broad definition that encompasses a wide variety of government activity. Nearly everything government does, from basic regulation to any form of taxation, influences markets at the margin. That market conditioning occurs in general is obvious – any action that government takes has an influence on society. The "market" outcomes that we observe are not void of government influence, thus the scare quotes. When 600,000 new jobs are created in a given quarter, that job growth does not occur in a completely *laizes-faire* market system. Government activities influence economic decisions made by a multitude of individuals and firms, and some of these decisions are likely to influence the labor market in which new jobs are created.

There is no doubt that market conditioning occurs. Government activity unavoidably influences markets both directly and indirectly. The question is whether market conditioning is truly a mechanism for government influence on distributional outcomes. For market conditioning to have an influence on distributional outcomes, at least some policies void of explicitly redistributional goals must change market processes in some way that produces differential benefits to those who would be at the top or bottom of the income distribution without the intervention of government.[11] While all policies have market conditioning effects, this is not to say that all market conditioning actually influences distributional outcomes. Some policies may influence markets in a way that has no real effect on income inequality. Furthermore, some policies may condition markets in a way that increases inequality while others might condition markets in an equalizing fashion. If these

---

[11] These market conditionings could shift inequality either higher or lower. For inequality to be reduced, of course, market conditioning would have to benefit the poor more than the rich. As Johnston (2007) points out in his journalistic account, there are many government activities that explicitly redistribute toward the top of the income distribution.

countervailing market conditioning forces simply cancel one another out, then government would have no net impact on distributional outcomes via market conditioning.

Distributional outcomes can be influenced via market conditioning by any policy that affects how much income individuals receive in labor and investment markets. For a real distributional impact, of course, these income effects must be distributed unevenly across society. There are two basic ways to influence income garnered through labor and investment markets. The first is by influencing the characteristics of individuals. If the labor market values intelligence, experience, skills, and so on, then the fortunes of those without these characteristics will improve if these characteristics can somehow be acquired with government assistance. The second is by influencing the market itself. If government takes action that induces demand for or supply of a particular kind of worker or changes investment rules, distributional consequences might be felt.

I will return in a later chapter to the question of whether the sum total of government policy has a systematic impact on distributional outcomes via market conditioning. In this chapter, my goal is simply to demonstrate that a wide array of government policies have the potential to influence income inequality via a market conditioning mechanism. In fact, some programs that do not explicitly redistribute income nevertheless have obvious distributional consequences. Nearly any governmental influence on market outcomes has the potential to influence income inequality, but a few specific examples are useful for illustrative purposes.

Education and Workforce Development

The clearest example of policies that influence the characteristics of individuals in a way that would have likely distributional consequences is public education and training programs. To conceive of the distributional impact of public education, we must first imagine a world in which public education does not exist. In this hypothetical world, people would obtain formal education only if they could pay for it or find a private entity willing to provide it to them. Needless to say, those with economic means would find it much easier to obtain education than those with little in the way of financial resources. This is the real situation in some countries today and was more closely approximated early in U.S. history. The bottom line is that, to the extent employers and other actors in the labor market value the skills produced by formal education, those able to obtain it will be more likely to get ahead economically than those without it.

With the public provision and funding of education, however, the situation changes markedly. Rather than leaving people to fend for themselves, public education provides the means for those at both the top and the bottom to gain basic and valuable skills. Even with public education, of course, some obtain more or better education than others, and not all of these educational differentials are rooted in divergent preferences.[12] Some who would like to obtain more education may not be able to, but publicly providing a basic level of education levels the playing field with regard to economic opportunity. It is, of course, important to note that even if everyone received the exact same amount of education, there would likely still be many differences that would produce unequal outcomes. But educational attainment would not be one of these differentiating factors.

Whether and how much public education is provided has obvious distributional consequences. In a hypothetical society where high levels of public education are available and no one is inhibited from educational achievement based on preexisting economic means, economic outcomes are likely to be more equal than in an alternative society in which education must be purchased like any other private service.

The difference between a society with no public education system and a society like the contemporary United States with an extensive system of public education is stark in terms of the expected distributional outcomes. Real political decisions, however, are not typically about whether or not to have public education, but about how much should be provided and what portion of the cost should be borne by the public. It is no longer a matter of serious political debate, for example, whether elementary education should be provided by the public. The structure and existence of funding for higher education, on the other hand, is often the subject of political disagreement. At this point in time,

---

[12] Oftentimes, for example, funding levels for education in poor areas are much lower than in more affluent areas. While there is debate about the degree to which funding translates into student performance, funding inequities are often present even in public programs that provides important benefits to middle and lower income families.

government is committed to the provision of primary and secondary education but takes only limited action in the form of programs like Pell Grants and student loan programs to provide education beyond high school.

Given that this book is about the influence of national policy on income inequality, public education might seem a strange choice as an example because it remains true that the lion's share of policy decisions regarding public education occur at the state and local level. There are, however, a variety of public education programs and policies undertaken at the national level. The *No Child Left Behind* initiative is a recent example of a national effort to level the educational playing field. If the ostensible goal of this legislation is achieved, gaps in educational outcomes across geography, economic circumstance, race, and ethnicity will be reduced. If this occurs, it should have implications for future distributional outcomes. Importantly, the heart of the potential redistributional effect is not in the form of direct payments to individuals or households. The effect comes through building skills and knowledge that will be valued in the marketplace, with the idea being that those who would otherwise not be valued by the market when they seek employment will be valued because of the implementation of NCLB.

Modifying the future marketability of today's fifth graders can clearly only condition future market outcomes. NCLB might also have current market conditioning effects via its impact on companies that provide educational testing services. The fact that standardized testing is one of many requirements in the NCLB legislation means that companies providing related services stand to benefit. It is interesting to note on this point that President George W. Bush's younger brother, Neil, began a company in 1999 that sells software designed to improve student performance on standardized testing. This is market conditioning – with somewhat opaque distributional consequences.

When it comes to illustrating the distributional effects of national education policy, an even more tangible example is useful – the Pell Grant program. Pell Grants are available to low income individuals to use for expenses related to higher education. A portion of the distributional effect of Pell Grants comes via explicit redistribution. Individuals receive money that they can use for educational expenses, and this program is funded through general tax revenue. This is the explicitly redistributional aspect of the program. But Pell Grants also open the door of opportunity to thousands of students each year. Without this program, some students currently receiving a college education would doubtlessly be unable to pay for college. In some cases, this might simply mean going to a more affordable institution, but for others it would mean missing out on a college education altogether.

The redistributional effects of Pell Grants are immediate and obvious, and were in fact accounted for in the previous section under the category of educational assistance. If I were to account for the explicitly redistributional effect of Pell Grants treated separately, the effect would be small. The program simply is not large enough in terms of expenditures to have a massive impact on the distribution of income. But there are additional distributional consequences of this program via market conditioning. The effect through this mechanism is not immediate, but occurs over a longer time frame. Access to education via Pell Grants will enable current students to earn more – much more – in the labor market in the years to come.

The Pell Grant program illustrates two important points. First, programs like this that aim to promote education and workforce development (or any form of skill development) have potential distributional implications because they provide participants with marketable skills that will have a return in increased income at some point in the future. Second, explicitly redistributional programs like Pell Grants often have secondary effects that occur via the market conditioning mechanism. Medicare, as another example, redistributes from rich to poor. This is the direct effect of the program. But it indirectly influences the incomes of doctors and health care providers by inducing demand (and payments) for services that many poor, elderly persons would not seek or pay for otherwise.[13]

Regulatory Policy

Regulations enforced by the Securities and Exchange Commission, Environmental Protection Agency, Food and Drug Administration, or

---

[13] One could argue that the reimbursement levels for Medicare participants is relatively low. Regardless, many of these patients would produce absolutely no economic return for health service providers were it not for government programs such as these. On the other hand, Medicare reimbursement rates also have consequences for the price of procedures performed outside of the Medicare system.

any other regulatory agency of the federal government are aimed at producing different outcomes than would be produced by a completely free and unregulated market. Some of these regulatory policies could have distributional effects.

One regulatory issue that has received some attention in the media is the expensing of stock options. For many years, companies were permitted to provide their employees with stock options at no charge to their profit/loss statements. In essence, corporations could provide stock (that could be sold by the employee at some time in the future) without having any current effect on their balance sheet. This strategy was useful for a variety of reasons. First, providing stock to high-level managers provided a strong incentive for these executives to keep the company on course over the long-haul by tying their economic well-being to that of the company's stock price. Second, it provided start-up companies, especially tech firms, with a low-cost tool to attract talented employees. These firms might not be able to pay a great deal in current salary, but they could provide the opportunity for future riches if the company succeeded.

While stock options are not completely costless to a company, in that there are future costs to a company issuing these options, the immediate costs are much less than expanding payrolls. This was the case, at least, until a recent regulatory decision that now requires the expensing of stock options – that is, subtracting a current valuation of stock options from current profit statements. Such a regulatory change may have the future impact of lessening income inequality by limiting the often massive income supplements that come to employees when they exercise stock options.

A multitude of other regulatory policies have important economic implications that could influence inequality and, at the very least, change the relative standing of employees and business owners situated in certain segments of the economy. A new environmental initiative, for example, to allow logging in certain previously protected areas will doubtlessly have an effect on logging corporations and their employees. Whether such initiatives would increase or decrease income inequality has no clear answer, but the economic well-being of loggers will likely be enhanced.

The post-9/11 emphasis on security also provides a good example of market conditioning, and homeland security initiatives have already provided a boon to security firms and industries providing security-related goods and services. Entirely new companies have sprung up marketing new technologies to increase homeland security. Small companies have increased revenue by marketing products to law enforcement. Salient Stills', which is a video-enhancement provider, began as a spin-off from the Massachusetts Institute of Technology Media Lab marketing its VideoFOCUS product to media outlets seeking to enhance images for publication. The company currently markets its product as a tool for law enforcement, security, military, and intelligence, significantly expanding its market beyond media providers such as newspapers and internet sites. Of course the new focus on security has spawned millions of dollars in new contracts for traditional defense contractors as well.

Social Policy

Social policies also produce outcomes that diverge from those of a hypothetical free market. Though the regulation of abortion is not often discussed in distributional terms, it is likely a mistake to remove distributional issues from the discussion completely. Abortion policy has no explicitly redistributive component (except to the extent that governments provide funding for abortions to low-income women, which does not happen in the United States at the national level). But it is not void of potential distributional consequences.

The availability of abortion may well have an equalizing influence in the economic realm. A pregnancy is full of economic implications. It certainly increases medical expenses in the short term and in the long term if the fetus is brought to term and remains with the mother after birth. But expenses are not of any concern when the emphasis is on income inequality. A pregnancy has income implications as well. In the short term, giving birth almost always requires time away from work. In the long term, again if the fetus is brought to term and raised by the parent(s), having a child forces some into difficult economic choices. How many hours can I work and still be a good parent? How much time can I reasonably expect to take off from work to deal with child care, doctors' visits, and other aspects of raising a child? The stakes of these questions become particularly important for those at the bottom of the income distribution.

Imagine a single, 20-year-old woman who is pregnant with her first child. Perhaps she is attending college and has a seemingly bright economic future. How would having the child influence her? She might not be able to complete college. This in and of itself hurts her prospects for future economic prosperity. After having the child she has to find work, but childcare is expensive and it may be hard to find a job with the kind of flexibility that is so often needed by someone raising a child on her own. Of course this is an extreme example. At least some women in this situation would have support from family or friends that could alleviate some of these problems, but the bottom line is that an unplanned pregnancy has the potential to derail future economic prospects. While adoption would be an (often complicated) option regardless of abortion policy, permitting the termination of this woman's pregnancy also alleviates threats to a bright economic future. Restricting abortion has economic consequences for pregnant women, and it is an impact that would likely be felt most strongly by low-income single women with few social support structures.[14]

CONCLUSION

This chapter has discussed two mechanisms through which government can influence distributional outcomes – explicit redistribution and market conditioning. Explicit redistribution is the mechanism that is most commonly considered as an influence on distributional outcomes. In the first part of the chapter, I described several redistributional programs and showed their substantive impact on income inequality in the year 2000. When we focus on explicit redistribution, the programs that matter most are not welfare programs targeted toward the poor. The programs that redistribute the most are those that could best be described not as redistributive welfare programs but as general social insurance provision – Medicare and Social Security. The reason these programs redistribute so much is that they are large programs targeted toward the elderly – a demographic group that earns little in the market due to their age.

---

[14] This is by no means meant as a defense of abortion, which is a complicated ethical and moral issue. The only point is that even a policy such as abortion, that on its face has nothing to do with redistribution, can nevertheless have distributional consequences.

The market conditioning mechanism, however, receives much less attention as a mechanism for distributional impact. I argued that everything government does has a direct or indirect effect on the economy. The economic outcomes that are produced by the market are only in part produced by free market forces and in part induced by governmental action. If government did not exist, nearly every economic interaction that we observe would likely be different and produce different outcomes. The level of economic inequality that we observe prior to the effects of taxes and transfers is essentially government conditioned market inequality.

The real question in the context of this book is whether these market conditionings that occur whenever government takes action of any kind actually produce a systematic influence on distributional outcomes. I began to answer this question by briefly discussing a few areas of policy that are not explicitly redistributive but have likely consequences for the current or future distribution of income. Policies designed to enhance the workforce influence the characteristics of individuals in such a way as to increase their value in the labor market. These policies also affect the supply of skilled laborers. Regulatory policies advantage some industries over others and almost certainly have marginal effects on any person connected with the affected industry. Finally, even social policies like abortion can be construed to influence distributional outcomes.

The discussion in this chapter just begins to scratch the surface. I have by no means conducted an exhaustive discussion of every government policy that might influence income inequality.[15] To the contrary, my goal in this chapter was simply to demonstrate that policies that do not explicitly redistribute income could influence income inequality via other mechanisms.

Notably missing from this chapter is any quantification of the distributional impact of these market conditioning policies. This is because the marginal effects of such policies are impossible to capture because we do not know how the world would look in the absence of all government action. This would be the baseline for comparison needed to quantify effects, but it is not observable. An additional issue is that the

---

[15] Page and Simmons (2000) discuss a variety of programs such as these in much greater detail.

distributional effects of many of the market conditioning programs are so marginal that it would be hard to parse out the influence of an individual program or policy. I return in Chapters 4 and 5 to the question of whether market conditioning has a systematic influence on income inequality. In the next chapter, I discuss some of the basic political divisions surrounding income inequality, distribution, and redistribution in U.S. national politics. What government does influences distributional outcomes, but how is the battle over "who gets what" structured? This will take us one step closer to answering the question of how political and distributional dynamics are linked.

3

Political Conflict over "Who Gets What?"

When we examine a cross-section of income data, as in the previous chapter, it is obvious that government programs have a tangible impact on who has how much money in America. Government action matters, but I am most interested in the political conflict that produces this government action. Government's impact on inequality, occurring through a variety of policy mechanisms, does not just happen, appearing out of nothing. It is likely a systematic product of politics. If we think of politics as the conflict over which values government will authoritatively enforce or the battle over who gets what, it is obvious that who wins and who loses in political conflict should alter the distributional outcomes that are in part determined by government policy. In this chapter, I examine the nature of political conflict over distributional outcomes in the United States. How might politics, as opposed to programs, influence income inequality?

Since at least the time of FDR and the Great Depression, modern American liberals have placed an intrinsic value on economic equality and have generally favored government action to balance the scales between the rich and the poor. Conservatives, on the other hand, do not find economic inequality to be an inherent societal problem and are less favorable toward government action that balances the scales of inequality. This is not to say that conservatives are unconcerned with the plight of the poor or lack compassion toward those less fortunate, but liberals are clearly more supportive of government action to reduce inequality, while conservatives believe the free market should determine distributional outcomes. The questions I address in this chapter are how these theoretical ideological differences manifest themselves in political decision making and whether ideological disagreement extends beyond debate over explicit redistribution to the more amorphous distributional consequences of market conditioning.

In order to shed light on these questions, I present two types of evidence in this chapter. In the next section, I examine the debate over the marriage "penalty" tax in some detail to flesh out how liberals and conservatives, Democrats and Republicans, operationalize their theoretical differences on distributional questions – in this case, on an issue in which popular accounts placed distributional concerns at the periphery. While few should doubt that Republicans and Democrats differ in their positions on issues of taxation, the marriage penalty debate is an interesting case because it was not a general tax package with readily apparent distributional implications. Nevertheless, distributional concerns were inserted into the debate. After discussing the marriage penalty tax, I turn to a more systematic examination of distributional attitudes in the House of Representatives, utilizing evidence from a survey of the 106th House conducted during the summer of 2004.

A CASE STUDY IN DISTRIBUTIONAL DEBATE: THE MARRIAGE TAX "PENALTY"

The debate over the marriage tax "penalty" began to gather momentum after the Republican takeover of Congress in 1994. The marriage tax "penalty" refers to a situation in which two people pay more in federal income taxes as married filers than they would if they were unmarried individuals. Consider the following example, presented in detail in first two columns of Table 3.1, which is based on tax law as it existed in 2000. Joe and Mary both earn about $30,000 per year. If Mary and Joe are not married, their individual tax liability would be $3,420 each. If married, their joint tax liability would be $7,474 (both assuming standard deductions). Joe and Mary pay $634 less in combined taxes as unmarried individuals than they would as a married couple. This is a marriage tax "penalty."

This shows one way in which tax law in 2000 (and for several years before) violated the concept of marriage neutrality. The ideal of marriage neutrality in a tax system is that two single individuals should

TABLE 3.1. *Marriage Bias in the Federal Income Tax*

| | Couple 1 | | Couple 2 | |
	Joe	Mary	Sam	Karen
As Individuals				
Income	$30,000	$30,000	$60,000	$0
Personal Exemptions	$2,800	$2,800	$2,800	$2,800
Standard Deduction	$4,400	$4,400	$4,400	$4,400
Taxable Income	$22,800	$22,800	$52,800	$0
Tax Calculation				
15% $0–$26,250	$3,420	$3,420	$3,938	$0
28% over $26,250	$0	$0	$7,434	$0
Total Tax	$3,420	$3,420	$11,372	$0
As a Couple				
Income	$60,000		$60,000	
Personal Exemptions	$5,600		$5,600	
Standard Deduction	$7,350		$7,350	
Taxable Income	$47,050		$47,050	
Tax Calculation				
15% $0–$43,850	$6,587		$6,587	
28% over $43,850	$887		$887	
Total Tax	$7,474		$7,474	
Marriage Penalty (Bonus)	$634		($3,898)	

Note: Calculations assume standard deduction and ignore effects of Earned Income Credit.

pay no more or less in taxes if they become married. In other words, a marriage-neutral tax system would have no economic influence on decisions regarding marital status. I place the scare quotes around penalty in the example above because the tax system as it existed in 2000 not only created penalties for some married couples, but also created bonuses for others. Another example, in the third and fourth columns of Table 3.1 will serve to illustrate the marriage "bonus." Sam earns $60,000 per year and Karen earns nothing. As an individual, obviously Karen would have no tax liability. Sam, however, would owe the IRS $11,372. If Sam were to marry Karen, however, their joint liability would be only $7,474. This is a $3,898 gain to Sam for becoming married. In this case the marital status bias is positive rather than negative.

In terms of statutory structure, there are literally dozens of provisions in the federal income tax that generate bias toward marital status, but the three largest contributors to marriage bias are the standard deduction, the width of tax brackets, and the phase-out rate of the Earned Income Credit (EIC) for individuals vis-à-vis married couples (General Accounting Office). Other contributing factors include the tax treatment of Social Security income and the Alternative Minimum Tax.

The income split, or the proportion of family income that each spouse earns, is the determining factor in whether or not marriage bias in the tax code produces a bonus or penalty. Couples with an even income split generally pay the largest penalties, while the largest bonuses accrue to single-earner couples. For example, in 2000, the standard deduction was $4,400 for an individual and $7,350 for joint returns. One reason the couple with an even income split from above (Joe and Mary) pays a marriage penalty is that they would be able to deduct a total of $8,800 if filing as individuals. The penalty in this case is created because the standard deduction for married couples is not twice that for individuals. For the single-earner couple above (Sam and Karen), however, there is a bonus because their deduction moves from $4,400 to $7,350 with no change in their aggregate income. This example is based on the standard deduction, but a similar set of results is produced by the width of income tax brackets. When a tax bracket is not twice as wide for a married couple as opposed to a single individual, single-earner couples will receive a bonus and those with a more even income split will pay a penalty. This is the case because couples with only one earner can claim two personal exemptions even if only one spouse is earning.

So, a lack of marriage neutrality in the tax code clearly existed during the 1990s. By virtue of being taxed as a unit, some couples paid a marriage penalty and others received a bonus. During the mid-1990s some Republican members of Congress began to argue for changes to the tax code that would eliminate the marriage penalty (but not necessarily the bonus).[1] A wide array of legislation was introduced aimed at the marriage penalty. A few more details regarding how these marriage penalties and bonuses came into existence will aid in understanding the

---

[1] Interestingly, laws preventing gay and lesbian couples from wedding create a situation in which they cannot suffer a marriage penalty or bonus. So, eliminating penalties and maintaining bonuses shift the tax burden to unmarried individuals, including gays and lesbians, some of whom would like to be married but are unable to legally do so.

various proposals targeted at the marriage penalty that were considered in the late 1990s and early 2000s.

A Brief History of Marriage Bias in the Federal Income Tax

One way to discuss the history of federal income tax law as it relates to marriage bias is to focus on three forms of equity – marriage neutrality, progressivity, and equal taxation of couples with equal earnings. Marriage neutrality, as discussed above, means that a couple will pay no more or less in aggregate taxes as a couple than they do as individuals. Progressivity refers to the idea that those with higher incomes should be taxed at a higher rate than those with lower incomes. Equal taxation of couples simply means that married couples with the same amount of money should pay the same amount in taxes. As we will see, these goals cannot all be achieved at the same time.

A 2001 Congressional Research Service Report utilizes an example that illustrates the tension between these three goals quite well (Esenwein 2001). We can go back to our four individuals from Table 3.1: Joe ($30,000 income), Mary ($30,000 income), Karen (no income), and Sam ($60,000 income). If these four were treated strictly as individuals, then progressivity would dictate that Joe and Mary earning $30,000 would each be taxed at a lower rate than Sam earning $60,000. Marriage neutrality dictates that if Mary and Joe become married and Sam and Karen also get married, each couple's combined tax liability would remain the same as it did when unmarried. But the third goal, equal taxation of couples with the same amount of income, dictates that both couples should pay the same amount of tax on their $60,000 of combined income. This would create a situation in which Sam is paying tax at the same rate as both Joe and Mary, and this runs counter to the ideal of progressivity. The CRS report summarizes the situation as follows:

Regardless of how these three concepts of equity are juggled, under current definitions an income tax can be designed to achieve any two of these goals, but it cannot achieve all three. The system might be marriage-neutral and tax couples with equal incomes equally but it could not be progressive. As an alternative, the tax system might be progressive and tax couples with equal incomes equally but then it would not be marriage-neutral. Finally, the tax system could be progressive and marriage-neutral but not tax couples with equal incomes equally (Esenwein 2001).

The balancing of these three goals in the U.S. federal income tax has not been constant over time. When first implemented in 1913, the federal income tax required each individual to file separately. That is, married couples filed as two individuals. Divergent property laws in different states, however, created advantages for some couples under this system. Specifically, married couples from common law states were required to treat their incomes separately. Couples in states with community property laws, however, could divide their income between the two spouses. In community property states, then, a couple could reduce their total tax liability by evenly splitting their income and thus subjecting the higher-earning spouse's wages to a lower marginal rate. In terms of the three forms of equity, this system was marriage-neutral and progressive (at least in common law states) but did not tax couples with equal earnings equally (Esenwein 2001).

The Revenue Act of 1948 created the basic structure of the tax system currently in place. In an effort to insure equal taxation of couples residing in different states with the same amount of income divided between spouses in the same way, Congress modified the tax code to create different tax rate schedules for singles and married couples. Deductions were larger and the tax brackets were wider for married couples than for singles so that, regardless of whether a couple was in a common law or community property state, they would pay the same amount of federal income tax. While this change in the tax code created equal taxation of couples with equal incomes, it introduced marriage bias into the tax structure. Many individuals (depending on the income level of their prospective spouse) could reduce their tax liability by getting married. So, the Revenue Act of 1948 created the first marriage bonus in the federal income tax.

For single individuals, however, this change could just as easily be called a singles penalty as a marriage bonus. Many people thought it unfair that a single woman paid more in taxes than a married man earning the same amount. Vivien Kellens, on behalf of the War Widows of America, testified before the Ways and Means Committee in the late 1960s that she unfairly paid a penalty due to the lack of suitable men created by deaths in World War II. This, in part, led to the 1969

Tax Reform Act. This modification of tax law aimed to ensure that no single individual would pay in excess of 20 percent more in taxes than a married couple with the same income. This was accomplished by widening tax brackets for individuals. It also meant, however, that some married couples paid more as a couple than they would as separate individuals. This was the first marriage penalty. Thus, the Tax Reform Act of 1969 did not really reduce marriage bias as much as it shifted the bias to fall more on married couples than before the reform.

Two important changes in the income tax occurred during the 1980s – one set of changes resulted from the Economic Recovery Act of 1981 and the other resulted from the massive tax code overall in 1986. Both of these changes had implications for marriage neutrality. Armed with the knowledge that only couples with two earners paid marriage penalties, the Economic Recovery Act of 1981 included a deduction for married couples equal to 10 percent of the lower earning spouse's income, not to exceed $2,000. While this did eliminate the penalty for some (but not all) couples, it also increased the bonus for other couples. This change also reintroduced the problem of not taxing couples with equal earnings equally because a single-earner couple would owe more in taxes than a dual income couple with the same income. The 1986 Tax Reform Act had implications for marriage neutrality indirectly, via a major change in progressivity. Reducing fourteen tax brackets to two and increasing the standard deduction for joint returns more than for individual returns reduced progressivity and the marriage bias. A variety of other provisions in this major tax overhaul also influenced marriage neutrality. With the 1986 Act, the two-earner deduction created in 1981 was repealed, contributions limits to Independent Retirement Accounts were different for married couples and individuals, and new deductions for the elderly and the blind were a function of marital status. So, the Tax Reform Act of 1986 increased marriage neutrality through reductions in progressivity, but also increased marriage bias through a variety of provisions dependent on marital status.

Changes in the early 1990s moved the structure of the income tax toward its pre-1986 form. After the Omnibus Budget Reconciliation Act of 1993, the tax code returned to five brackets and greatly expanded the Earned Income Credit, thus increasing structural progressivity at the expense of marriage neutrality. So, it was in this context –

some couples paying marriage penalties and others receiving bonuses – that the Republicans took over Congress after the 1994 mid-term elections. One of their targets was the marriage penalty. Over the next several years, proposals to eliminate marriage penalties were repeatedly offered, and partisan differences over this issue demonstrated divergent perspectives on government's role in distribution and redistribution.

Targeting the Marriage Penalty in the Post-Republican Revolution Congress

After the Republican takeover of Congress beginning with the 104th Congress convening in 1995, efforts to eliminate the marriage tax penalty began to gain momentum. Still, while some Republican members of Congress had been proposing legislation targeted at reducing or eliminating the marriage penalty for several years, tax relief for married couples was not the most immediate priority to Republican leaders in the House and Senate. The first successful efforts to provide substantial tax relief to married couples came during the 106th Congress when the Marriage Penalty Tax Relief Reconciliation Act of 2000 (H.R. 4810) was passed by both the House and Senate. President Clinton, however, vetoed this measure. After the election of George W. Bush, the Congress again took action on tax relief for married couples, and this relief became law when President Bush signed the Economic Growth and Tax Relief Reconciliation Act of 2001. I will focus on the 2000 debate because it was focused specifically on the marriage penalty, whereas the 2001 debate was more general due to the fact that it was motivated by the broad tax cuts proposed by George W. Bush.

The marriage penalty tax would not seem at first blush to have a great deal to do with distributional outcomes. Of course any tax legislation has the potential to change distributional outcomes, but marriage bias in the federal income tax does not seem to naturally pit the rich against the poor. This, in fact, is one of the reasons I have chosen to present the marriage penalty tax as a case study – it is not a natural case for distributional debate. As we will see, however, even this debate brought disagreements about distribution and redistribution into focus. Examining the debate that occurred surrounding these legislative efforts to reduce the marriage penalty provides insight into partisan differences on distributional questions.

The Marriage Tax Debate in 2000

Various strategies were proposed to deal with the marriage penalty, ranging from providing special deductions for two-earner families, to increasing the phase-out point of the Earned Income Credit for married couples, to widening tax brackets and increasing standard deductions, to making single filing optional. Notably absent from any of the legislative proposals were tax code changes that would have achieved marriage neutrality. Most of the proposals only partially eliminated marriage penalties, kept marriage bonuses intact, and actually increased the tax rates of unmarried individuals relative to married couples.

While dozens of bills aimed at the marriage penalty were introduced, in the end the debate came down to one strategy presented by the Republicans and two alternatives presented by the Democrats. The basic strategy of the Republican proposal (H.R. 4810, S. 2839) was to increase the phase-out point of the Earned Income Credit for married couples, increase the standard deduction for couples to twice that for singles, and widen the 15 percent tax bracket for married couples to twice that of singles.[2] The House Democratic alternative (H. AMDT. 571) was similar to the Republican proposal except that it did not widen the 15% tax bracket and made the implementation of the tax cut contingent on Social Security and Medicare trust fund surpluses as well as national debt projections. Senate Democrats in 2000 presented optional single filing as a way to completely eliminate marriage penalties, but this option was to be phased out for couples with over $100,000 in taxable income (S. AMDT. 3863).

Before taking a more detailed look at the rhetoric surrounding this issue, it is useful to understand the real distributional implications of the plans. The clearest way to compare the main Republican and Democratic alternatives is to examine how much couples at various points in the income distribution benefit from the tax reductions. Table 3.2 clearly shows that the House Democratic plan favored those at the middle and bottom of the income distribution much more than the Republican plan. This is due to the fact that the Republican plan included widening of the 15 percent bracket and the Democratic plan did not. Widening even the lowest tax bracket provides the greatest

---

[2] This is the same basic strategy that eventually became law in 2001.

TABLE 3.2. *Tax Cuts (in $billions) to Married Couples at Specified Levels of Taxable Income*

| Income | House GOP | | | House Dem | |
	Deduction and EIC	Bracket Widening	Benefits (%)	Deduction and EIC	Benefits (%)
<$10K	$0.0	$0.0	0.1	$0.0	0.3
$10–20K	$0.5	$0.0	2.0	$0.6	8.8
$20–30K	$1.2	$0.0	5.0	$1.4	20.9
$30–40K	$1.0	$0.0	4.1	$1.1	16.3
$40–50K	$0.9	$0.0	3.8	$0.9	14.3
$50–75K	$1.6	$2.9	18.5	$1.6	25.2
$75–100K	$0.6	$6.6	29.4	$0.6	9.4
$100–200K	$0.3	$6.7	28.5	$0.3	4.0
>$200K	$0.1	$2.1	8.6	$0.1	0.9

Source: Center for Tax Justice.

absolute benefits to those with moderately high incomes because this widening is identical to a marginal tax rate cut for those previously in the second (28 percent) tax bracket or higher. The differences between the Senate Republican and Democratic plans (data not shown) are even more clearly distributional in nature because the initial Republican proposal by Senator Roth (DE) widened not only the 15 percent tax bracket but also the 28 percent bracket, while the Senate Democrats' alternative explicitly made marriage penalty reductions contingent on income levels.

The basic argument of Republicans was an appeal to fairness and equity in the tax system – two individuals should not have to pay higher taxes as a married couple. Congressman Jerry Weller (IL) clearly articulated the Republican position in a floor statement on July 12, 2000 (*Congressional Record* H5859-60):

We have often asked in the House Chambers, many of us, is it right, is it fair that under our Tax Code 25 million married working couples, on average, pay almost $1,400 more in higher taxes just because they are married. Now, is that right, is that fair, that if a couple chooses to participate in the most basic institution in our society, marriage, that they are going to pay higher taxes if they work? Unfortunately, under our Tax Code, that is true. If a husband and wife are both in the workforce, both the man and the woman are in the workforce, a two-income household, under our Tax Code they will file jointly and, because of that, they will pay a marriage tax penalty. That is just wrong. We have made this a priority, to eliminate the marriage tax penalty suffered by 25 million married working couples.

While the Democrats agreed in principle with reducing marriage penalties, they objected to the Republican strategy for three primary reasons. First, the Republican plan provided tax cuts to couples even if they were paying no tax penalty. Second, the size of the tax cut decreased revenue to an alarming degree in the eyes of Democrats. Finally, they had distributional concerns that are fairly obvious from the table presented above. These concerns were summarized by Congressman Sander Levin (MI) on the same day during the debate of H.R. 4810 (*Congressional Record* H5860):

I favor a marriage penalty tax relief bill. That is why I say to my colleague on the Committee on Ways and Means, I am for the Democratic substitute, and I can face the thousands of voters in my district, whose numbers the Republicans like to cite for each of us in the House. We know our districts, and I know this bill that I am supporting; the Democratic substitute is the answer. ... First of all, half of the relief in their bill goes to those who do not pay a marriage penalty. So they attach the marriage penalty label, though more than half of the money does not apply to that situation. Secondly, many families with kids will not get the full relief that the bill promises because of the way they have shaped it. Thirdly, the lion's share, and this is important, of the money goes to the top quarter of the tax filers. Fourthly, look at the out-year projections. Assuming the AMT is eventually applied, and the chairman of the committee has promised that, the 20-year cost of their bill is $700 billion. That plays lightly with the future of my grandchildren and with the need to address Medicare and Social Security.

House Republicans were quick to point out, however, that the Democratic alternative not only failed to provide as much general tax relief as the Republican plan but also did less to reduce marriage penalties. While neither plan presented in the House was designed to fully eliminate marriage penalties, the fact that the Republican plan did more was incontrovertible. In the end, the Democratic alternative (H. AMDT. 571) was defeated 198 to 228, with just eight Democrats joining Republicans (Roll No. 390). H.R. 4810 eventually passed the House 269 to 159, with some bipartisan support for the final bill

(Roll No. 392). Clearly, however, the key vote on this piece of legislation was that on the Democratic alternative, and it was nearly a party-line vote.

Upon passage in the House, H.R. 4810 was taken up for consideration in the Senate, and the first action was the complete replacement of H.R. 4810 with an alternative (S. 2839) crafted by the Senate Finance Committee chaired by William Roth (R-DE). The Senate Republicans wanted to go even farther than the House version of the bill by not only widening the 15 percent tax bracket but also widening the 28 percent bracket for married couples. The Senate Republican proposal was designed to eliminate the marriage penalty for more couples and expand tax relief more generally for those not subject to marriage penalties. This proposal also meant that a greater proportion of tax relief would be given to couples at the top part of the income distribution and this plan generated more lost revenue than the plan passed in the House. Both of these factors raised the ire of Senate Democrats.

Unlike the House Democratic alternative, which was more constrained in its marriage penalty relief than the House Republican plan, the Democratic alternative in the Senate promised to completely eliminate the marriage penalty for most households. The essence of the Democratic plan in the Senate was optional single filing (S. AMDT. 3863). That is, couples could file either as individuals or as a married couple. If they would be subject to a marriage penalty when filing as a married couple, they could avoid the penalty by filing as two single individuals. On the other hand, those couples already receiving a marriage bonus could retain their bonus by continuing to file as a married couple. However, the Democratic plan was designed to phase out this single filing option as household adjusted gross income (AGI) rose above $100,000, with the benefit completely eliminated for those with AGI above $150,000.

Democrats argued that their strategy to reduce marriage penalties was preferable to the Republican plan for three primary reasons. First, the Democratic plan completely eliminated marriage penalties for households with less than $100,000 in annual taxable income. The Republican plan focused only on the largest culprits in the marriage penalty: the Earned Income Credit phase-out, standard deductions, and tax bracket width. Dozens of other provisions can create small marriage penalties, and the Republican plan did nothing to address these issues.

Second, the Democratic plan was less costly. This was the case because the Democratic plan gave tax cuts only to couples paying a marriage penalty while the Republican plan gave tax relief to couples regardless of whether they were paying a penalty or receiving a bonus. The Democratic plan also saved money by targeting the tax cuts to approximately the bottom 90 percent of households in the income distribution.

During the debate over the Republican and Democratic proposals, several interesting exchanges took place on the floor of the Senate. Senator Edward Kennedy (D-MA) made it clear that distributional matters were central to the Democratic opposition of the Republican proposal (*Congressional Record* S6792):

I want to be clear. I support legislation that would provide tax relief to the working families who are currently paying a marriage penalty. Such a penalty is unfair and should be eliminated. However, I do not support the proposal which the Republicans have brought to the floor. While its sponsors claim the purpose of the bill is to provide marriage penalty relief, that is not its real purpose. In fact, only 42 percent of the tax benefits contained in the legislation go to couples currently subject to a marriage penalty. The majority of the tax benefits would actually go to couples who are already receiving a marriage bonus, and to single taxpayers. As a result, the cost of the legislation is highly inflated. It would cost $248 billion over the next ten years.

And, as with most Republican tax breaks, the overwhelming majority of the tax benefits would go to the wealthiest taxpayers. This bill is designed to give more than 78 percent of the total tax savings to the wealthiest 20 percent of taxpayers. It is, in reality, the latest ploy in the Republican scheme to spend the entire surplus on tax cuts which would disproportionately benefit the richest taxpayers. That is not what the American people mean when they ask for relief from the marriage penalty. With this bill, the Republicans have deliberately distorted the legitimate concern of married couples for tax fairness....

...A plan that would eliminate the marriage penalty for married couples could easily be designed at a much lower cost. The House Democrats offered such a plan when they debated this issue in February. The Senate Democrats are offering such an alternative plan today. If the real purpose of the legislation is to eliminate the marriage penalty for those working families who actually pay a penalty under current law, it can be accomplished at a reasonable cost.

The key to drafting an affordable plan to eliminate the marriage penalty is to focus the tax relief on those couples who actually pay the penalty under current law. The Republican proposal fails to do this, and, as a result, it actually perpetuates the marriage penalty despite the expenditure of $248 billion on new tax cuts. Under the Democratic plan, the tax relief actually goes to those currently paying a marriage penalty. It is also essential to target the tax benefits to the middle income working families who need tax relief the most. The Democratic plan focuses the tax benefits on those two earner families with incomes less than $150,000. By contrast, major portions of the tax benefits in the Republican plan would go to much wealthier taxpayers at the expense of those families with more modest incomes. As a result, the Democratic proposal would cost $11 billion a year less, when fully implemented, than the Republican plan, yet provide more marriage penalty tax relief to middle income families.

The Republican response to these lines of argument brought the marriage penalty tax debate squarely into the category of a classic partisan debate over taxes. Republicans argued that their more costly plan was appropriate because taxes should always be reduced in a climate of budget surpluses. They also argued that marriage bonuses are a misnomer and giving tax relief to single-earner couples not paying a marriage penalty is wholly appropriate. Finally, they argued that targeting tax cuts away from the top of the income distribution is inappropriate. Senator Roth (R-DE) summarized the Republican argument as follows (*Congressional Record* S6802, S7105):

According to the Congressional Budget Office, in 1999, there were about 7.5 million joint returns with an adjusted gross income greater than $100,000. And 56 percent of that group, or 4.2 million couples, suffered from a marriage penalty. The total amount of marriage penalty suffered by those couples is almost $12 billion, which is more than one-third of all the marriage penalties caused by our Tax Code.

The average marriage penalty faced by each one of these families is about $2,800. Yet despite these significant marriage penalties encountered by these couples – and they claim that this is a targeted tax bill to eliminate the marriage tax – this substitute amendment [the Democratic alternative] turns its back on those taxpayers. The amendment tells these folks they make too much money and should not receive complete relief....

...I would ask those who oppose this family tax relief: Just how big will America's budget surplus have to get before America's families deserve to receive some of their tax dollars back? If not now, when? If eight percent of just the overpayment is too big a refund, how little should it be? How long do they have to wait? How hard do they have to work? How large an overpayment do they have to make? This bill is fair. We have addressed the three largest sources of marriage tax penalties in the tax code – the standard deduction, the rate brackets, and the Earned Income Credit. And we have done so in a way that does not create any new penalties – any new disincentives in the tax code.

We have ensured that a family with one stay-at-home parent is not treated worse for tax purposes than a family where both parents work outside the home. This is an important principle because these are important families....

... Families across America are waiting for us to make good on our promise. They are waiting for us to return some of this record surplus to them. Let's approve the Marriage Tax Relief Reconciliation Act of 2000 and let's divorce the marriage tax penalty from the tax code once and for all.

In the end, the Democratic plan was defeated on a nearly straight party vote, with one Republican (Lincoln Chafee, RI) joining with the Democrats (Record Vote 200). With the Democratic alternative defeated, the Republican proposal then passed the Senate (Record Vote 215) with weak support from Democrats. There were, however, some differences between the House and Senate version of the legislation that had to be reconciled in conference. The main differences between the two versions were that the Senate version expanded the 28 percent bracket while the House bill expanded only the 15 percent bracket and the Senate version phased in the tax cuts more quickly than the House version. The conference agreement discarded the 28 percent bracket expansion but phased the cuts in more quickly than the original House version. The conference version of the legislation passed the House on July 20, 2005 (Roll No. 418) and the Senate on July 27, 2005 (Record Vote 226), both with moderate bipartisan support.

The legislation was forwarded to President Clinton, but the president vetoed the legislation (by pocket veto), and in his remarks explaining the veto, distributional concerns were again raised:

H.R. 4810 would cost more than $280 billion over 10 years if its provisions were permanent, making it significantly more expensive than either of the bills originally approved by the House and the Senate. It is poorly targeted toward delivering marriage penalty relief – only about 40 percent of the cost of H.R. 4810 actually would reduce marriage penalties. It also provides little tax relief to those families that need it most, while devoting a large fraction of its benefits to families with higher incomes.

Taking into account H.R. 4810, the fiscally irresponsible tax cuts passed by the House Ways and Means Committee this year provide about as much benefit to the top one percent of Americans as to the bottom 80 percent combined. Families in the top one percent get an average tax break of over $16,000, while a middle-class family gets only $220 on average. But if interest rates went up because of the congressional majority's plan by even one-third of one percent, then mortgage payments for a family with a $100,000 mortgage would go up by $270, leaving them worse off than if they had no tax cut at all. We should have tax cuts this year, but they should be the right ones, targeted to working families to help our economy grow – not tax breaks that will help only a few while putting our prosperity at risk.

The rhetoric on both sides of this debate was no doubt overheated, with Republicans invoking images of middle-income couples toiling under the weight of a government-imposed marriage penalty and Democrats bemoaning an untargeted tax cut benefiting primarily the wealthy. Given that upper income households pay a large proportion of federal income taxes, it was somewhat misleading for Democrats to label the Republican proposal as slanted toward the rich. Senator Roth's statement regarding the proportionality of tax cut benefits to the aggregate taxes paid by income groups is well-taken. A tax cut that benefits income groups in equal proportion to their tax burden will inevitably benefit the rich more than the poor. The fact remains, however, that the Republican plan was more favorable to those at the upper part of the income distribution than was the Democratic plan. Republicans simply favored a more general tax cut than did the Democrats, and this fact has distributional consequences that were a prevalent part of the debate in both the House and the Senate. Eliminating the marriage penalty does not inherently invoke distributional issues. Both the policy proposals and the rhetoric surrounding these proposals, however, became intertwined with concerns about distributional consequences. It seems clear from this perhaps somewhat unlikely example, then, that determining who gets what is an important aspect of political conflict in the United States.

SYSTEMATIC EVIDENCE OF THE PARTISAN AND IDEOLOGICAL DIVIDE OVER DISTRIBUTIONAL OUTCOMES

The debate over the marriage penalty provides a useful case study in distributional disagreements between the major U.S. parties. The marriage tax penalty was not, at the outset, an obvious distributional issue. The marriage penalty did not fall on one income group to the exclusion of others. But even in this case, the parties developed very different strategies for reducing marriage penalties, with different distributional implications. In this case, it is clear that Republicans were much more willing to extend the benefits of tax relief to those at the top of the income distribution than were Democrats. While the marriage penalty debate is a good illustrative example, it may not generalize to other policy debates. Thus, in this section, I present some data evidencing partisan and ideological divergence on more general distributional attitudes. The goal of this section, like the last, is to show how Republicans and Democrats and conservatives and liberals differ in their attitudes about income distribution and what government can and should do about it. But the evidence I present here is broader than that discussed above. I analyze general attitudes rather than a specific policy proposal.

I focus on assessing the distributional preferences of Democratic and Republican members of the U.S. House of Representatives. While members of the House are political elites, they are not necessarily the leaders of intellectual movements (though some are). House members make policy, and as policymakers, their views are shaped not only by intellectual tradition and pure ideology, but also by the practical considerations that are necessary for policymaking. Thus, the House of Representatives is an excellent population in which to test the proposition that the preferences of Democratic and Republican policymakers align in a practical sense with commonly accepted theoretical distinctions between liberalism and conservatism. In order to compare the attitudes of Republicans and Democrats and liberals and conservatives on matters relating to distributional outcomes and government's role in shaping these outcomes, the strategy I followed was to ask members about their attitudes and preferences by conducting a survey in summer 2004.

Surveying Members of the 106th House

The largest hurdle in conducting a survey of the House is obtaining responses. Most Congressional offices have a blanket policy of not responding to surveys, and members of the House are obviously busy people with a limited amount of time. I utilized three strategies to obtain as many responses as possible. First, I utilized a survey format that would take little time to complete and would provide the members the greatest flexibility in participation. Specifically, I designed a short, two-page questionnaire that could be completed and returned to me by mail. The full questionnaire is available in Appendix A. Second, I sought help from members with whom I had a personal or professional connection. One member agreed to sign a letter of support encouraging colleagues to participate in my study that was included with the survey materials. Finally, I delivered the questionnaire to each House office in person. In each case, I sought to speak with the highest ranking member of the staff in order to explain my project and what I was requesting from each member. In many cases I was able to meet with the member's chief of staff, and in most cases was able to meet with someone ranking at least as high as legislative director.

Questionnaires were successfully delivered in person to the offices of every member of the House between July 1 and July 8, 2004. The final response rate was just under 10 percent.[3] Clearly, with just 435 members in the House, this response rate makes statistical analysis challenging. Because of the small number of respondents, the results discussed below should only be viewed as suggestive, and no solid conclusions can be reached. But as becomes clear below, interesting and suggestive patterns nevertheless emerge.

The primary purpose of this survey is to compare the attitudes of Republicans to the attitudes of Democrats. In order to make such comparisons, it is necessary to confirm that Republicans and Democrats who responded to the survey do not differ systematically from their co-partisans who did not respond. For example, if only very liberal Democrats and very conservative Republicans responded to the survey, then partisan differences on distributional attitudes would likely be magnified in the survey data. To assess my ability to make reasonable cross-party comparisons with data from this survey, I examine the correspondence of characteristics between those who responded to the questionnaire and those who did not. Specifically, I compare the ideological positions of respondents to nonrespondents, measured with roll-call voting behavior.

These data, which are presented in Table 3.3, lead to the conclusion that potential response bias does not interfere substantially

---

[3] The overall response rate appears to be very low but is not substantially lower than some mail surveys of the general public. As an even better point of comparison, only 40 percent of members responded to a survey conducted in 1973 by a subcommittee in the House itself – the Intergovernmental Relations Subcommittee of the House Committee on Government Operations (Stenberg and Walker 1977). Democrats responded at a higher rate than Republicans, which is likely due to the fact that the letter of introduction was provided by a Democratic member. My hope was to provide a letter of introduction from a member of both parties, but despite my best efforts could not secure help from any Republican members.

TABLE 3.3. *Comparison of Respondents and Full House Characteristics*

Characteristic	Respondents	Full 106th House
Percent Republican	32%	51%
Chamber DW-NOMINATE Average	−0.15	0.05
Republican DW-NOMINATE Average	0.46	0.46
Democrat DW-NOMINATE Average	−0.43	−0.39

with comparisons across party. Given that the goal of the analysis discussed below is to observe correlations between distributional attitudes and ideology and to compare partisan preferences on these issues, the most important findings here are in the third and fourth rows of the table. The ideology of Republican (and Democratic) respondents closely mirrors the ideology of all Republican (and Democratic) members when analyzed by party. Thus, conclusions about differences between Republican and Democratic House members can likely be made without fear of problems created by nonresponse bias.[4] While this is reassuring, the small sample size still makes statistically significant differences difficult to find, and all the results from this survey should be viewed as illustrative, rather than definitive. In addition, it is clearly not appropriate to generalize from this sample to the entire House, since Democrats were much more likely to respond than were Republicans. The only inferences I seek to make, however, are comparisons across party.

Results of the House Survey

In discussing the results generated by the House survey data, I focus on four potential sources of partisan disagreement regarding distributional and redistributional policymaking. The first potential

---

[4] It is unlikely with a response rate of less than 10 percent that the data analyzed here have the properties of a random sample. Members of the House self-selected into the sample. Democrats were more likely to respond than Republicans. However, it appears that participation within party was random with respect to ideology. Moderate Republicans were no more likely than conservative Republicans to participate in the survey. The same is true of Democrats. Still, because of the low response rate, the results discussed in this section should only be viewed as suggestive. However, what they suggest turns out to be interesting, as the discussion below demonstrates.

source of disagreement is substantive preferences regarding how much inequality should exist in society. It is possible that Democrats and Republicans fundamentally disagree about how much income inequality should exist in the ideal society. The second potential source of disagreement is over the level of priority that income inequality should be given vis-á-vis other economic outcomes. The time of policymakers and the resources of government are scarce, so even if Democrats and Republicans agree about the level of inequality that should exist, policy differences will be more likely to occur if Democrats place a higher priority on reducing income inequality than do Republicans. The third potential source of disagreement is the theoretical role of government. Policy disagreement regarding income inequality could simply be a part of broader ideological disagreements about the appropriateness of government intervention in the economy. The fourth potential source of disagreement that I address is group-based. That is, Republicans and Democrats might produce policies with divergent distributional consequences because of the types of groups that each party views as deserving of government aid.

Substantive Preferences Regarding Income Inequality

In order to gain traction on the question of whether there is partisan disagreement about how much inequality should exist, in one section of the questionnaire I presented each respondent with a list of ten occupations. The list included very low paying jobs as well as jobs that currently garner very high wages – computer programmer, construction worker, janitor, CEO of a Fortune 500 company, fast food employee, physician, plumber, factory line employee, human resources manager, and certified financial planner. I asked the members to report how much the average person in each occupation should earn annually, regardless of how much a person in that occupation actually earns.[5] This measurement approach avoids the charged issues of inequality and redistribution and instead asks direct questions about wages outside of the distributional context.

Table 3.4 compares Democratic and Republican members of the House on their preferred salary level for ten occupations. Overall, the

---

[5] This measurement strategy closely resembles one developed and reported in Verba and Orren (1985).

TABLE 3.4. *Partisan Differences in the House Regarding Preferred Salary Levels*

	Salary ($1,000s)			
	R	D	Difference	Significance
Occupation				
Computer Programmer	54.3	62.6	8.3	0.26
Construction Worker	42.1	50.2	8.1	0.13
Janitor	28.7	33.5	4.8	0.25
CEO of Fortune 500 Company	650.0	600.0	−50.0	0.81
Fast Food Employee	21.1	25.4	4.3	0.16
Physician	267.9	286.6	18.7	0.85
Plumber	53.6	54.3	0.7	0.92
Factor Line Employee	35.9	44.8	8.9	0.11
Human Resources Manager	55.4	68.6	13.2	0.12
Certified Financial Planner	89.3	77.4	−11.9	0.38
Summary Measures				
Average Lowest Income	20.4	25.4	5.0	0.09
Average Highest Income	650.0	602.3	−47.7	0.81
Median Income	50.2	57.3	7.1	0.28
Highest/Lowest	33.4	26.1	−7.3	0.44
N	7	22		

Note: Statistical significance results are from a two-sample *t*-test of the null hypothesis that Republican and Democratic members of Congress have the same salary preferences.

most striking aspect of the data presented here is the similarity between members of opposing parties. Even using a lenient 0.10 as the level of statistical significance, there are no discernible differences between Democrats and Republicans regarding how much they think specific jobs should pay. In fact, there is not even a single discrepancy between Republicans and Democrats about the relative position of particular occupations. Members of both parties agree that, of the occupations listed, fast food employees should earn the least, CEOs should earn the most, and every other occupation should hold the same ranking relative to other jobs.

The most important results in this table, however, are at the bottom, where I present summary measures. Differences between Republican and Democratic income distribution preferences are at most slight, but a pattern does seem to emerge. Democrats prefer higher incomes for the lowest paid occupations (significant at 0.10 level) and the average of all occupations than do Republicans. Republicans, on the other hand, prefer higher salary levels than Democrats for the most highly paid occupations. The ratio of the highest salary to the lowest salary is the most direct indicator of distributional preferences. The average high to low ratio for Republicans was 33.4, meaning that the typical Republican respondent expressed a preference for the highest paid occupation to earn over 33 times the amount earned by the lowest paid occupation. The corresponding number for the Democrats was 26.1. These numbers suggest that Democrats prefer less income inequality than Republicans. Given the lack of significance, it would be a mistake to overinterpret these results, but considering the sample size the basic pattern that emerges makes it impossible to ignore the possibility that Republicans and Democrats have at least slightly different substantive preferences regarding income inequality.

Relative Importance of Reducing Income Inequality

The evidence on partisan disagreement about preferred levels of inequality is weak at best. Democrats in the House may prefer slightly lower levels of income inequality than Republicans, but the differences are certainly not striking. Given the small differences across party lines on substantive distributional preferences, other sources of policy disagreement are more important. One such source of policy divergence is partisan differences over the relative importance of reducing income inequality as a goal of government action. The policies crafted in the U.S. House are designed to influence myriad social and economic outcomes. It is quite possible that while Republicans and Democrats have only slight differences of opinion regarding the ideal level of income inequality, they nevertheless tend to enact policies with divergent distributional consequences due to differences of opinion about the relative importance of reducing income inequality as a policy goal. The expectation is that reducing inequality is more important to Democrats than Republicans.

The evidence supporting this expectation is unequivocal. As part of the questionnaire, members of the House were presented with seven policy goals: increasing labor productivity, decreasing unemployment, increasing economic growth, decreasing income inequality, increasing international trade, reducing poverty, and controlling inflation. They

TABLE 3.5. *Partisan Differences in the House Regarding Seven Economic Outcomes*

Economic Outcome	Average Ranking			
	R	D	Difference	Significance
Increasing Labor Productivity	3.67	5.24	−1.57	0.000
Decreasing Unemployment	3.17	2.04	1.13	0.016
Increasing Economic Growth	1.25	2.72	−1.47	0.004
Decreasing Income Inequality	6.42	3.32	3.10	0.000
Increasing International Trade	4.33	6.32	−1.99	0.000
Decreasing Poverty	4.58	2.44	2.14	0.000
Controlling Inflation	4.83	5.84	−1.00	0.026
N	12	25		

Note: Statistical significance results are from a two-sample t-test of the null hypothesis that Republican and Democratic members of Congress rank the specified economic outcome as equally important.

ranked these goals from most to least important. Table 3.5 shows the average ranking of each goal for Republicans and Democrats and presents a test of the significance of any differences. The difference between Republicans and Democrats is statistically significant for the ranking of each and every policy goal. Democrats rank decreasing unemployment, income inequality, and poverty higher in importance than Republicans. The most important goal for Democrats is decreasing unemployment. Republicans, on the other hand, rank increasing labor productivity, economic growth, international trade, and controlling inflation higher than Democrats. The clear choice for most important goal among Republicans is increasing economic growth.

If we focus for a moment on the differences across parties, decreasing income inequality generates by far the most disagreement between the parties, though decreasing poverty also evidences partisan divergence. Republicans almost uniformly rank decreasing income inequality near the bottom, at 6.42 out of 7, while Democrats see the goal of equality as moderately important, at 3.32. The goal of decreasing income inequality clearly stands out as a subject that generates strong conflict along party lines and provides empirical support for the idea that Democrats and Republicans have different distributional and redistributional policy preferences.

Theoretical Role of Government

An additional source of disagreement between the parties regarding distributional policy springs from divergent views on the theoretical role of government. As mentioned earlier, liberals and conservatives, Democrats and Republicans, do not completely agree on government's proper role in society. Democrats are usually described as much more willing than Republicans to support economic intervention by government. If these general ideological disagreements about government intervention in the economy extend to the specific outcome of income inequality, which is also a more important issue for Democrats, this would be a clear source of policy disagreement between the parties.

In order to learn about lawmakers' normative views of inequality and government's role in influencing it, I presented members of the House with five statements and asked them to report their degree of agreement with each statement. These five statements along with the mean level of support for each statement within each party are reported in Table 3.6. The first two statements in the table return to preferences on distributional outcomes, but rather than assessing these preferences by asking about preferred income levels of specific occupations, here the opinions are more abstract in nature. The results indicate that Republicans and Democrats both generally agree that society is better off when income inequality is reduced, though Democrats agree much more strongly than Republicans. Interestingly, this first item is the only one on which Republicans and Democrats are not on opposite sides of the midpoint, with members of both parties essentially on the same side. The clearer disagreement relates to the necessity of inequality for a strong economy. This item generates the largest absolute difference between the parties. Democrats are not willing to concede that inequality is necessary for a strong economy, while Republicans are strongly convinced that this is the case.

The next statement in the table taps preferences regarding general government intervention in the market, and the responses evidence strong and statistically significant differences between the parties. When framed in a very general way, Democrats agree that government must sometimes intervene in the market to ensure the best economic outcomes while Republicans disagree.

The final two statements are designed to assess attitudes toward government intervention specific to distributional outcomes. The first

TABLE 3.6. *Partisan Differences in the House Regarding Distributional Preferences and State Intervention to Increase Equality*

Statement	Average Response (1 = Strongly Disagree, 7 = Strongly Agree)			
	R	D	Difference	Significance
Society is better off when the income gap between the richest and poorest individuals is reduced	4.2	6.4	2.2	0.000
Differences in income between the richest and poorest individuals in society are necessary to ensure a strong economy	5.1	2.3	2.8	0.000
To ensure the best economic outcomes, government must sometimes intervene in the market	3.1	5.8	2.7	0.000
It is inappropriate for government to implement programs that redistribute income from the rich to the poor	4.2	2.8	−1.5	0.095
Government has a responsibility to modify some market processes in order to provide equal economic opportunities to all citizens	3.0	5.7	2.7	0.000
N	11	25		

Note: Statistical significance results are from a two-sample t-test of the null hypothesis that Republican and Democratic members of Congress have the same average response to each statement.

of these statements asks about explicit redistribution – one of the mechanisms of policy impact outlined in the previous chapter. Attitudes toward explicit redistribution are somewhat surprising at first blush. While the difference between Republicans and Democrats attains marginal statistical significance, the absolute difference between the parties on this item is the smallest of the five. The difference between the parties is much more stark for the next item, which examines attitudes toward intervention in market processes to ensure equal economic opportunity. Here we see a large and statistically significant difference between Republicans and Democrats, with Democrats favoring intervention to produce equal economic opportunity and Republicans opposing such action.

These results on preferences for redistribution and equalizing economic opportunity are the two most interesting findings from the House survey. Given the broad acceptance of the importance of equal economic opportunity in the United States, it is surprising that a statement relating to economic opportunity generates more partisan disagreement than a statement about explicit redistribution. The statement on explicit redistribution refers specifically to redistribution from the rich to the poor, but that is precisely the kind of redistribution that is most commonly done by the national government. If Republicans and Democrats do not disagree strongly on explicit redistribution from the rich to the poor, then they do not disagree about the kind of redistribution that is typically most explicitly on the table in policy debates.

When it comes to distributional outcomes, Republicans are often described as the party of economic opportunity and Democrats are described as the party of redistribution. In reality, however, government must often take action to provide equal economic opportunities. Republicans are reticent to support such action. When any form of state action is required, it turns out that Democrats are the party of both redistribution and economic opportunity. These results also have an important implication for the analyses that will be conducted in later chapters. Specifically, I will examine whether partisan and ideological conflict has a larger impact on income inequality via the explicit redistribution mechanism or the market conditioning mechanism. These results suggest that the effect via market conditioning may prove more important.

Group-Based Politics

A final kind of disagreement between the parties that could lead to divergent distributional and redistributional policies is differential support for benefits to different groups in society. The differences that we have seen so far between Republicans and Democrats could be further

TABLE 3.7. *Partisan Differences in the House Regarding Government Provision of Benefits*

Should Provide Benefits To	Average Response (1 = Strongly Disagree, 7 = Strongly Agree)			
	R	D	Difference	Significance
Stockholders	3.6	2.8	−0.8	0.190
The Aged	5.2	6.3	1.1	0.004
Small Businesses	4.3	4.8	0.6	0.259
The Poor	4.5	6.5	2.0	0.000
Veterans	5.3	6.2	0.9	0.029
Corporate Executives	2.6	1.6	−1.0	0.035
Children	4.7	6.6	1.9	0.000
Doctors	3.2	3.1	−0.1	0.891
N	11	25		

Note: Statistical significance results are from a two-sample *t*-test of the null hypothesis that Republican and Democratic members of Congress have the same average response to each statement.

augmented if Democrats favor benefits to social groups that tend to be toward the bottom of the income distribution and Republicans favor benefits to groups that tend to be at the top. Table 3.7, which reports the degree to which Republicans and Democrats in the House report support for "explicit government benefits" to a series of groups, finds mixed support for this conclusion.

Democrats are more supportive of benefits to the aged, the poor, veterans, and children than are Republicans. Republicans, on the other hand, are more supportive of benefits only to corporate executives (although CEOs are still the least deserving of support according to Republicans). The largest difference between the parties occurs on support for benefits to the poor. So, there is some evidence that Democrats are more favorable toward benefits to groups at the bottom of the income distribution and Republicans are more supportive of benefits to those at the top. However, it is important not to overstate the substantive significance of these results. There are no statistically significant differences between the parties in support of benefits to stockholders, small businesses, and doctors. Furthermore, there is no group for which the parties are on opposite sides. Republicans might be more in favor of benefits to corporate executives than are Democrats, but even Republicans view such benefits negatively. On the other side of the coin, Republicans and Democrats both have a generally favorable view of benefits to the aged (a group at the bottom of the income distribution), but Democrats are simply more favorable.

CONCLUSION

In sum, it is clear that distributional matters are an important component of partisan and ideological conflict. In theory, conservatives are much less apt than liberals to favor government action designed to balance the scales of inequality. In practice, these theoretical distinctions are borne out in policy debates and reported preferences. We saw in the marriage penalty tax debate of 2000 that even a policy debate on a matter not inherently connected to distributional concerns nevertheless evidenced an ideological divide over income inequality. Republicans favored a plan that was more generous to families at the top of the income distribution than the plan favored by Democrats. Tentative evidence from a survey of House members showed even more stark differences between the parties. Republicans and Democrats appear to have different priorities when it comes to distributional outcomes, and they are divided over government's role in influencing income inequality. Republicans are likely to oppose any action which modifies market outcomes in a way that benefits the poor more than the rich. In this way, Democrats are more favorable toward government activity that would balance the scales of inequality through market conditioning. Likewise, Democrats are more amenable to programs that explicitly redistribute income from those who have more to those who have less. The question to which I turn in the next chapter is whether these partisan and ideological differences translate into predictable economic outcomes. That is, do political dynamics influence the path of income inequality over time?

4

Party Dynamics and Income Inequality

This chapter marks a turning point in the story of equality and inequality in America. To this point, I have examined inequality and the politics of inequality through a cross-sectional lens. The degree of inequality, who has the money, what government does to influence inequality, and partisan and ideological differences regarding inequality have been examined using one snapshot frozen in time at the dawn of the twenty-first century. This chapter marks a change in perspective from the static to the dynamic. From this point forward, I will examine movement in income inequality over time and will utilize time series methods to accomplish this task. This change in perspective will provide the capability to examine not just what government does or does not do about inequality, but whether macro political change has influenced the path of income inequality in the United States. By shifting to a cross-temporal analytical perspective, I will assess whether political dynamics are connected to the dynamics of income inequality. For some readers, the simple promise of exploring the connection between politics and income inequality is likely to generate interest in this research. But analyzing the connection between political dynamics and income inequality also sheds light on existing theories and provides opportunities for developing new explanations about the connections between politics and economics.

A THEORY OF DISTRIBUTION AND REDISTRIBUTION IN THE
UNITED STATES

My examination of the influence of political dynamics on distributional
outcomes is rooted, first, in the macro politics model of American
politics. The macro politics model presents an aggregate portrait of
several portions of U.S. politics that were traditionally examined at
the micro level. Research in the macro politics tradition examines phenomena such as issue attitudes, voting behavior, partisanship, and
policymaking activity. But instead of approaching these issues from the
perspective of individual citizens, elites, or policy decisions, the macro
politics tradition focuses on electorates, branches of government, and
the ideological direction of policy. Perhaps most importantly, many
aspects of government and politics that were once examined in isolation are examined as part of a complex yet orderly system. In the macro
politics tradition, the behavior of the electorate, the Congress, the president, and the courts are interconnected. Analyzing these connections
is at the heart of the macro politics model.

One of the central arguments advanced in the macro politics model
is that public opinion influences policymaking (Erikson et al. 2002,
Stimson et al. 1995). This connection exists, according to the theory, because elected officials who fail to pay adequate attention to
the mood of the public can be replaced at regular intervals via elections. Thus, these officials are sensitive to the desires of the public and
attempt to enact policy following the general contours of public opinion between elections. When they are unable or unwilling to behave
in line with public preferences they are replaced with politicians who
will. In other words, policymaking responds to public opinion due to
both electoral turnover and changes in the behavior of elected officials
between elections.

The policies made by the national government are the ultimate object
of explanation in existing studies of the U.S. macro polity. Aside from
feedback from policy outputs to mass behavior and preferences, the
impact of public policy on society is not central to most research in
this tradition. In the next chapter, I directly extend the macro politics
model to societal outcomes by exploring the connection between policymaking and distributional outcomes. For the moment I set public
policy aside to focus on an earlier stage in the macro political process

– the partisan composition of government. The question I examine in this chapter is whether and how party control of the major policy-making institutions of government influences distributional outcomes in the United States. The analysis in the previous chapter leads to clear expectations regarding the effects of party control on distributional outcomes – Democratic control should lead to more egalitarian outcomes and Republican control should produce the opposite. These predictions are certainly connected to the macro politics model, but the primary theoretical emphasis in this chapter is power resources theory.

Power Resources, Partisan Politics, and Income Distribution

My examination of partisan dynamics and distributional outcomes in the post–World War II United States is rooted in and builds on the power resources theory of the welfare state. Power resources theory applies a class-centric theoretical lens to welfare state development. Such a class-based perspective on the welfare state may seem an odd place to start an analysis of distributional outcomes in the United States, given the widespread perception of the United States as a society in which class is relatively unimportant.[1] Nevertheless, power resources theory contains useful insights that lead to specific, testable empirical hypotheses regarding the connection between political dynamics and distributional outcomes.

As originally formulated, power resources theory was proposed as an alternative to the pluralist and corporatist/Marxist theories of politics (Korpi 1983). The pluralist perspective argued that interest aggregation occurs readily such that all groups in society can influence the state and, via this influence, generate outcomes in line with their interests. The corporatist perspective, on the other hand, placed class at the forefront. Under this view, the state is not an entity that can be accessed by all members of society. Capital holders have immense advantages, meaning that the lower classes cannot use the state to produce outcomes favorable to their interests. The welfare state, instead, is a tool used by the capitalist class to maintain the status quo and prevent revolution by the lower classes.

---

[1] Though see recent work by McCarty et al. (2006) and Stonecash et al. (2002) on the increasing importance of class in American politics.

According to power resources theory, both the corporatist and pluralist perspectives are only partially correct. Power resources theory agrees with the Marxist supposition that class is important, but takes exception to the idea that capital holders have so complete an advantage in terms of power that the lower classes are impotent to tip societal outcomes in their direction. At the same time, although power resources theory embraces the idea of pluralism that the political system is open to multiple interests, the theory eschews the early pluralist notion (Dahl 1967, Truman 1951) that class is a relatively minor dimension along which interests are organized. In borrowing from both Marxist and pluralist theories, power resources theory combines the two into a new view of the state, with important implications for understanding welfare state activity and distributional outcomes.

Power resources are the central concept in power resources theory. As defined by Korpi (1985), power resources are "attributes (capacities or means) of actors (individuals or collectivities), which enable them to reward or punish other actors" (p. 33). Some specific power resources would include control over the means of production, money, occupational skills, education, and labor capital. Importantly, these power resources can be latent resources that are not always active. In democratic societies the lower classes have a substantial potential for power resource mobilization. They can form interest groups, labor unions, and are more or less free to protest. To the extent that lower class power resources are actualized, society can be changed in a way that aligns with the interests of the lower classes. Importantly, the actualization of lower class power resources is not constant across societies or over time within societies.

The idea that the power resources of the lower classes, or more precisely the actualization of these resources, can vary within and across societies became central to the application of power resources theory to the welfare state. The theory focuses on two general types of lower class power resources – market and political. Market power resources exert influence on private decisions made within labor, investment, and other markets. A wage earner with a particular job skill, for example, is endowed with power resources in part because she or he could withhold their labor from a business owner. Workers with low skill levels would have fewer power resources than workers with highly specialized skills because the former are easier to replace than the latter. Political power resources relate to decisions made by the state. Individuals have greater political power resources when they can effectively influence state policy to shift outcomes toward their interests. Those who are organized, for example, have greater political power resources than those who are not.

The power resources literature has focused on one primary indicator of market power resources and one indicator of political power resources. Lower class *market* power resources are actualized through labor unions, while the actualization of lower class *political* power resources occurs through organization in left parties. With reference to market power resources, consider the plight of a single wage earner. Even a highly skilled wage earner with a relatively high level of individual power resources when compared to other individual wage earners is typically at an extreme resource disadvantage in the market compared to his or her employer. The major market power resource available to a single wage earner is the ability to quit working and thus deprive the employer of labor. A threat by only one worker to walk off the job would rarely if ever pose a serious threat to the employer. As individuals, wage earners tend to be lower in the wage distribution than those for whom they work, and thus have little in the way of bargaining power against their employer. Furthermore, such workers are easily replaced so the threat of quitting has little influence on the employer. The threats of individual wage earners would be expected to have little effect on private-market decisions of employers.

When workers can bargain collectively instead of as individuals, however, their power resources can be more fully actualized. While the threat of one worker walking off the job is likely of little consequence to a business owner or manager, the threat of an entire group of workers leaving is much more serious. Replacing one worker is simply much easier than replacing 5,000. The unionization of a group of workers provides for such a collective bargaining system. Labor unions can ostensibly represent the interests of an entire group of workers, providing them much greater bargaining power. Power resources can be further enhanced when labor unions from different industries or with different skill sets can cooperate. The ability of workers to unionize and cooperate with one another once unionized should influence employers' private-market decisions by increasing the wages, benefits, and other remunerations provided to workers over and above what would be received in the absence of unions. Thus, *power resources theory predicts that union strength reduces market inequality* by increasing the wages and benefits of those at the bottom of the income distribution.

Political power resources, on the other hand, are related to the ability to influence what government does. Market decisions clearly have an impact on the well-being of members of society, but the state is in a unique position to affect societal outcomes. Having the power of the sword and the purse allows the state to take from some and give to others. The state also has the power to protect property from unlawful taking by one citizen from another. The degree to which the state utilizes its legitimate use of force to protect current property holders as opposed to redistributing property of various types has important implications for the relative well-being of the rich and the poor. According to power resources theory, the state can be used as a tool of the lower classes to improve their well-being. For lower class political power resources to be actualized, the lower classes must organize to influence state activity.

While the actualization of lower class power resources can occur in a variety of ways, from community organizations to political interest groups to candidate recruitment, the power resources literature places a particular emphasis on organization in left political parties. According to the theory, those at the bottom seek to influence the state by aligning themselves with political parties that represent the interests of those at the bottom of the income distribution. This emphasis on parties is an additional way in which power resources theory diverges from the pluralist argument. The pluralist view emphasizes organized interests, such as interest groups. These organized interests influence state action directly and via their influence within political parties. In power resources theory, however, political parties are viewed as the most important determinant of state activity. Political parties take center stage in power resources theory, in large part because parties are the most proximate and direct indicator of lower class power resources in government. The central prediction of power resources theory with regard to political power resources, then, is that *left party control produces greater redistribution by the state.*

In the view of power resources theory, interest groups, campaign dynamics, and individual candidates might marginally influence the ability of the lower classes to actuate their interests through public policy, but political parties in government have the most direct ability to craft policy outcomes. While in the context of the United States it would be a mistake to completely ignore the effects of organized interests, in this chapter I will adhere to the classic power resources emphasis on political parties as a measure of political power resources (Bradley et al. 2003, Stephens 1979). This will only be the case in this chapter. In the next chapter I present a modification of power resources theory that moves beyond analyzing parties alone, and examines public policy itself as an indicator of lower class power in government. This will account for the myriad power resources that shape public policy in addition to political parties.

In sum, power resources theory argues that lower class power resources will affect distributional outcomes at two stages. First, market power resources influence the market distribution of income. When labor unions are strong, the distribution of income produced by private market decisions should be more egalitarian because labor unions will increase the bargaining power of wage earners versus capital holders, thus enabling those at the bottom of the income distribution to extract more from those at the top. Second, political power resources influence state activity. When left parties control government, the state should have a greater equalizing impact via explicit redistribution than it does when right parties are in charge.

Assessing the Evidence on Power Resources Theory

Early empirical tests of power resources theory focused on the mobilization of lower class power resources, the bargaining power of wage earners versus business owners, and the size of the welfare state. Korpi's (1978) earliest analysis examined Sweden as a case study for power resources theory, showing that economic organization of the lower classes produced greater employment opportunities and that political organization under the banner of Social Democracy produced greater welfare state redistribution. Later, the argument was extended by examining cross-national data on lower class mobilization in unions and left parties, showing that countries with greater actualization of lower class power resources implemented more redistributive social policies and experienced more labor strikes (Korpi 1983). Stephens (1979) also provides early cross-national evidence in favor of power resources theory by demonstrating that labor organization and strong left parties are associated with higher amounts of domestic spending and greater income equality.

At about the same time that power resources theory was being applied to welfare state development, two important competing theories became prevalent as well. The logic of industrialism thesis argued essentially that economic development and demographic change drive welfare state development within and across countries (Wilensky 1975). The state-centric theory of welfare state development, which sprang from the work of Heclo (1974) and Skocpol (1979), argued that state structure as well as the attitudes and capacity of bureaucrats determine the rate at which a sizable welfare state can emerge.

Analyses of these competing theories of the welfare state generated divergent results. For example, in a time-series, cross-sectional analysis of eighteen developed democracies, Hicks and Swank (1992) find evidence that left and center party governments produce greater welfare expenditures. However, Pampel and Williamson (1988) argue that party control of government has essentially no independent effect on welfare spending. Both of these studies focused on explaining welfare expenditures, and examining other indicators of welfare state effort only adds to the lack of consistent findings (Esping-Andersen 1990, Korpi 1989, Myles 1984). Huber et al. (1993) made important strides in explaining the divergent findings in previous studies. They also generally found strong support for the thesis that party control of government affects the welfare state. Despite what has been characterized as the dominance of power resources theory in the welfare state literature (Orloff 1996), more recent studies of welfare state effort have found support for all three traditional theories (Hicks 1999, Huber and Stephens 2001, Swank 2002) and have developed more complicated theoretical frameworks that attempt to integrate multiple explanations from the three traditions (Hicks and Misra 1993).

Most of the research mentioned to this point examines various measures of welfare state effort, such as the amount of social welfare expenditures. It is important to remember, however, that power resources theory is more centrally concerned with distributional outcomes as opposed to the size of the welfare state. The actualization of lower class power resources should influence state action, *and* this state action should tip the scales of inequality toward the poor. In other words, what the state actually does is more important for the theory than how big it is. This idea is implicitly acknowledged and partially examined in studies that assess welfare spending by category (Huber et al. 1993). Welfare state expenditures such as unemployment insurance have a much different distributive profile than programs such as income assistance. Unemployment insurance is typically designed to reproduce market inequalities by providing higher benefit levels to those with higher lost wages due to loss of employment. Income assistance programs, on the other hand, often provide benefits based on a formulaic determination of need rather than wage-earning history and are thus more redistributive. Still other programs provide a basic level of provision to all citizens regardless of need or position in the wage distribution. Differences in the distributive profile of welfare state programs explain why Social Democratic Party control produces more general state spending in the form of subsidized goods and services but is not correlated with the amount of transfer payments through programs like unemployment insurance, while Christian Democratic Party control produces greater transfer payments but not general growth in government (Huber et al. 1993).

Examining multiple measures of welfare state effort and expenditures by category based on their redistributive profile is useful, but still avoids a test of the true heart of power resources theory – distributional outcomes. Recent work has acknowledged that distributional outcomes provide the most pivotal evidence regarding power resources theory, and the advent of the Luxembourg Income Study (LIS) has provided data for truly comparable cross-national analyses (Bradley et al. 2003). Still other researchers have resolved the issue of the importance of outcomes over spending by focusing their attention on cross-temporal research within a single country, as I will here (Hibbs and Dennis 1988, Kelly 2005).

Using LIS inequality data, Bradley et al. (2003) provide substantial cross-national evidence in favor of power resources theory. One important contribution of this work is its analysis of distributional outcomes in two stages. The first stage is pretax, pre-transfer income inequality. The second stage is redistribution by the state. Both of these stages are treated as distinct dependent variables. When testing power resources theory, explicit examination of distributional outcomes is clearly superior to analyzing the size or effort of the welfare state. But the two-stage conceptualization of distributional outcomes also moves beyond other studies that examine the distributional process in a single stage. Wallerstein (1999), for example, uses wage inequality as the object of explanation, while Hibbs and Dennis (1988) analyze posttax, post-transfer income inequality. Examining two stages of the distributional process provides a direct test of the two central predictions of power resources theory discussed above – that union strength decreases market inequality and that left party control of government increases redistribution.

The two-stage analysis by Bradley et al. (2003) shows that labor union strength influences market outcomes, while left party strength influences state redistribution. This is entirely in line with the predictions of power resources theory. Labor unions, as the actualization of lower class power resources in the form of wage-bargaining organizations, influence the distribution of income prior to government taxes and transfers. Strong labor unions equalize the distribution of pretax, pre-transfer income inequality. On the political side of the coin, left party governments enact qualitatively different welfare states than parties of the right – strong left parties produce more government redistribution.[2]

Since posttax, post-transfer inequality is likely the most important single outcome of interest given that it is the final distribution of economic resources, it is important to note that the final product of the analysis of this two-stage conceptualization of inequality is examination of the final distribution of income. Posttax, post-transfer inequality is the final outcome of the two stages of the distributional process. Pretax, pre-transfer inequality plus redistribution generated by taxes and transfers produces posttax, post-transfer inequality. The value added of the two-stage conceptualization of distributional outcomes is that it provides additional theoretical leverage

---

[2] In the cross national context in which Bradley et al. (2003) are working, the religious nature of political parties also matters. They find that strong Christian parties produce less redistribution than non-Christian parties, regardless of their ideological stripe. This is an important finding, but one that is not particularly relevant for my analysis of the two U.S. parties.

by allowing separate analyses of market and state influence on distributional outcomes. This is particularly useful given that power resources theory explicitly identifies market power resources and political power resources as two pathways through which the lower classes can influence the distributional process.

Applying and Extending the Theory: Inequality in the United States

My goals in this chapter are to test the traditional predictions of power resources theory in the context of the post–World War II United States and to examine some still unverified implications of power resources theory. The two most fundamental hypotheses of power resources theory relate to the impact of market and political power resources on distributional outcomes. The primary impact of market power resources is expected to be in the market. Specifically, labor union strength should produce lower levels of market inequality. Political power resources, on the other hand, primarily influence state action. Thus, the prediction for political power resources is that left party strength will increase government redistribution. This latter hypothesis could be called the classic redistribution hypothesis of power resources theory, and it has been tested time and again in the cross-national literature.

I also develop an additional hypothesis of power resources theory that has failed to receive much attention, let alone support, in previous studies of welfare state expenditures and income inequality. I hypothesize a link between political power resources and market outcomes – an impact of political power resources on distributional outcomes via market conditioning in addition to explicit redistribution. Private individuals, corporations, and organizations are doubtlessly the ones who make the decisions that fundamentally drive market outcomes. These private decisions, however, are always conditioned by the institutions and policies created by government. I discussed some of the specific policies that have such a market conditioning impact in Chapter 2. State action influences market decisions, meaning that an outcome such as pretax, pre-transfer inequality is a combined result of private and state actions. While this does not inherently mean that both political and market power resources will influence such an outcome, power resources theory strongly suggests that they should. If lower class power resources are the driving force behind distributional outcomes, the goal of greater equality should be pursued through every possible mechanism. If the state can influence pretax, pre-transfer income inequality, which it likely can through a variety of policy mechanisms, then lower class political power resources in the form of left-party strength should produce not just more government redistribution, but also greater pretax, pre-transfer income equality.

This idea is not completely novel. Earlier studies in the power resources tradition have also suggested that such a connection is predicted. Huber et al. (1993) capture this idea, stating that "Social Democratic Parties and labor movements seek to shape the labor market itself..." (p. 717). But this was not central to their argument and, in fact, they argue that most of the market effect of political power resources would be captured by employment rates, with left parties pursuing full employment. Despite the theoretical possibility that left-party strength would influence market inequality, previous studies have not given much attention to testing this hypothesis, and the minimal evidence that is available on this point has not found a connection between party strength and market inequality. In a cross-national analysis, Bradley et al. (2003) estimate the connection between left parties and pretax, pre-transfer inequality and find a weak correlation, but the political power resources explanation of pretax, pre-transfer inequality could not be disentangled from the market power resources variables. The conclusion from their analysis is that market power resources are by far the more powerful determinant of market inequality, and political resources have no discernible independent impact. Others have provided similar evidence (Wallerstein 1999).

My theoretical focus is to examine the following two questions in the context of the post–World War II United States: (1) Does labor union strength and left-party control of government reduce market income inequality? and (2) Does left-party strength increase government redistribution? While support has been found for the central predictions of power resources theory, this support is not unequivocal. Analyzing the theoretical claims of power resources theory in the United States from 1947 to 2000 provides a particularly interesting context for analysis for several reasons.

First, the type of welfare state regime present in the United States may make it a least likely case for the applicability of power resources theory. According to the typology developed by Esping-Andersen (1990), the United States is a prime example of a liberal welfare state. Liberal welfare states typically provide benefits through means-tested programs, small universal transfer programs, and social insurance plans. When possible, liberal welfare states allow the market to allocate economic well-being. Because liberal welfare states rely so heavily on markets in the distributional process, the traditional predictions of power resources theory are less likely to be borne out in a liberal welfare state than in either social democratic (e.g., Sweden) or conservative (e.g., France) welfare states, which rely more heavily on public provision of welfare.

In fact, much of the existing literature on the American welfare state is explicitly devoted to explaining why the American case is so different from others. "American exceptionalism" is often the object of explanation for scholars of the U.S. welfare state (Alesina and Glaeser 2006, Iversen 2005, Lipset and Marks 2000, Lockhart 1991, Pontusson and Kenworthy 2005, Quadagno 1988, Skocpol 1992). Although arguments concerning the root causes of this exceptionalism vary, these studies make clear that the U.S. welfare state developed at a slower pace and is much smaller than its European counterparts. Given the exceptionalism of the American welfare state, questions regarding the ongoing causal dynamics of the U.S. welfare state are wholly legitimate. Power resources theory has found support in cross-national studies, but do the internal, cross-temporal dynamics of the exceptional American welfare state truly align with a theory primarily developed with reference to the European continent? It may, in fact, be the case that cross-national studies of welfare state dynamics often find support for traditional power resources theory hypotheses in spite of including the U.S. case rather than because of its inclusion. In other words, it may not be fully appropriate to generalize the cross-national evidence to cross-temporal variation in the U.S. welfare state.[3] If power resources

---

[3] Some cross-national studies, of course, rely on cross-temporal variation in addition to cross-national variation in a cross section. The question then becomes whether more explained variation is driven by cross-sectional or cross-temporal variation. Given the small number of time points typically available in the cross-national literature, it is reasonable to surmise that much of the variation that produces the results comes

theory truly applies to the American case, this would indeed be a strong vindication of the theory.

While the traditional predictions of power resources theory – that left party strength will increase state redistribution and labor movements will decrease market inequality – face a particularly strong challenge in a liberal welfare state with weak unions such as the United States, the more novel implication I have drawn from power resources theory that left-party strength will independently increase market equality may be more likely in a liberal welfare regime. Since liberal welfare states allow for market decisions to allocate economic well-being, policymakers in such regimes are likely to be more interested in crafting policies that work via a "market" mechanism than policymakers in social democratic or conservative contexts that are more accepting of redistributive programs. In fact, as we saw in the last chapter, it appears that there is greater political disagreement between the American parties with regard to market conditioning and the provision of economic opportunity than there is over explicit redistribution.

The U.S. context is also particularly interesting as a test of power resources theory due to the ideological positioning of the Democratic and Republican parties. While there should be no doubt that the U.S. parties diverge dramatically on their preferred policies (McCarty et al. 2006), neither party presents a truly *left* position when compared to European parties, perhaps due to the incentive to capture the median voter that is especially prevalent in a two-party system. The Democrats are a center-left party and the Republicans are fairly far to the right in the ideological distribution of parties around the world. This raises further questions about the degree to which power resources theory will yield correct predictions in the U.S. context. There is some evidence, however, that the major predictions of power resources theory could be supported within the United States. Hibbs and Dennis (1988), though not explicitly testing power resources theory, find that redistributive effort (welfare spending) is higher when a Democrat rather

from the cross-sectional variation across countries. Furthermore, even if a great deal of variation is present cross-temporally, none of the studies of which I am aware fully account for the possibility that the causal processes at play in the United States could be different from the other countries under examination.

than a Republican controls the White House. I ask whether this effort actually translates into redistributional impact.[4]

Finally, analyzing the United States is appealing due to the possibility of assessing distributional processes over a much longer period of time than is typical in existing studies. While cross-national analyses of welfare expenditures have examined data extending back in time as far as the 1950s, examinations of income inequality typically rely on data available only since the 1970s.[5] The problem with assessing income inequality since the 1970s is that the income distribution in nearly every country has been trending toward greater inequality. This creates questions about the empirical tests that have been applied. By examining income inequality over a longer time period, I am able to assess the causes of distributional outcomes during times of increasing and decreasing inequality. Analyzing a time period during which inequality has both risen and fallen provides for a more reliable empirical test of power resources theory versus competing explanations.

ASSESSING THE EFFECT OF MARKET AND POLITICAL POWER RESOURCES ON DISTRIBUTIONAL OUTCOMES

I test the degree to which classic indicators of power resources – labor movements and left party strength – influence the distribution of

---

[4] In addition, Bartels (2008) argues that Democratic Party strength in government decreases income inequality. While the results that I will report below are consistent with his analysis, my work differs in at least three important ways. First, Bartels does not place his results in the theoretical context of power resources theory. Second, Bartels analyzes inequality in money income. Recall that money income includes market income plus the redistributive effects of some government programs, but not all. For example, money income does not take account of any benefits that accrue to households via government health programs, nor does it account for the effect of taxes. This is not a small omission given the billions of dollars spent on such programs each year. Third, Bartels analyzes the distributional process in a single stage without separating market conditioning and explicit redistribution. My work focuses on power resources theory, analyzes two stages of the distributional process, and takes account of a broader range of redistributive programs. Thus, I am working with measures of the distributional process that allow for a much fuller accounting of the impact of government and a more nuanced assessment of the causal processes that produce government-conditioned market inequality and explicit redistribution by the state.

[5] Hibbs and Dennis (1988) provide one exception in their study of the United States, by analyzing data from 1950 to the late 1980s. Again, their theoretical focus is not on power resources theory.

income through two distinct yet related mechanisms: explicit redistribution and market conditioning. I utilize a two-stage conceptualization of distribution and redistribution similar to Bradley et al. (2003) to test the central hypotheses. Conceptualizing the distributional process in two stages motivates three concepts – pre-redistribution inequality, post-government inequality, and explicit redistribution. Pre-redistribution inequality is the amount of inequality that exists prior to government activity, in essence excluding income from government benefits. Post-government inequality is income inequality after taxes and benefits are accounted for. Explicit redistribution is the total impact of government on income inequality via taxes and benefits; essentially, it is the difference between pre-redistribution and post-government inequality. These concepts were introduced in the static, cross-sectional analytical framework of Chapter 2, but they remain useful in the dynamic, cross-temporal framework that I use in this chapter and those that follow.

Pre-redistribution inequality is operationalized as the pretax pretransfer distribution of income measured as a ratio of the aggregate income of the top 20 percent of households to the bottom 40 percent (T20/B40 ratio).[6] Specifically, this measure examines inequality in income (adjusted for underreporting) from the following sources as measured by the U.S. Census Bureau: earnings, private retirement income, private pensions, interest, dividends, rents, royalties, estates, trusts, alimony, child support, and outside assistance. Post-government inequality is inequality in posttax post-transfer income and is measured on the same scale as pre-redistribution inequality. Posttax post-transfer income includes pretax pre-transfer income, plus government cash and noncash benefits (unemployment compensation, state workers' compensation, Social Security, Supplemental Security Income, public assistance, veterans' benefits, government

---

[6] This measure is selected over other alternatives such as the Gini coefficient for two main reasons. First, most explicit redistribution is from the top quintile to the bottom two quintiles. Thus, it is important to focus on the top and bottom of the income distribution when examining explicit redistribution. The Gini coefficient and other similar summary measures place a great deal of emphasis on the middle of the income distribution when calculating income inequality rather than focusing on the areas of the distribution in which redistribution actually occurs. Secondly, the Census microdata necessary to calculate Gini and other summary inequality statistics is too crude prior to the late 1970s to calculate pre- and post-government income.

survivor benefits, government disability benefits, government pensions, government educational assistance, Medicare, Medicaid, and food stamps), minus federal taxes paid. Finally, redistribution is the percent reduction in inequality between pre-redistribution inequality and post-government inequality:

$$\left(\frac{\text{Pre} - \text{Post}}{\text{Pre}}\right) 100 = \% \text{ Redistribution} \tag{4.1}$$

More complete details on the creation of these measures are available in Appendix B.

The paths of pre-redistribution inequality, redistribution, and post-government inequality over time are charted in Figures 4.1, 4.2, and 4.3. The pre-redistribution inequality series charted in Figure 4.1 shows relatively steady levels of inequality from the late 1940s to the early 1970s, at which point a strong trend toward greater inequality is observed.[7] The year 1951 marked the low point of pre-redistribution inequality. In this year, the top income quintile had just 2.92 times as much aggregate income as the bottom two quintiles combined.

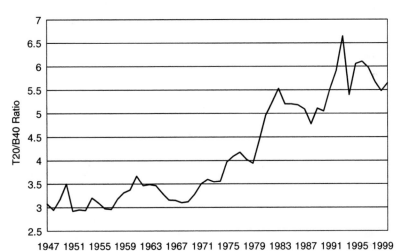

FIGURE 4.1. Pre-Redistribution Inequality: 1947–2000

[7] Inequality of money income actually declined between 1947 and the early 1970s, while we see that pre-redistribution inequality was stagnant. In both measures the late 1960s or early 1970s marked a turning point in the path of inequality.

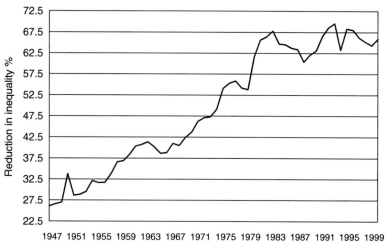

FIGURE 4.2. Redistribution: 1947–2000

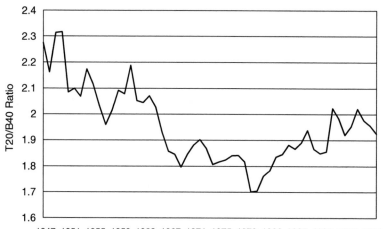

FIGURE 4.3. Post-Government Inequality: 1947–2000

By 1993, the T20/B40 ratio increased by more than twofold – the top quintile in that year had nearly seven times as much income as the bottom two quintiles combined.

That increase in inequality, however, was accompanied by an increase in the redistributive impact of government. Figure 4.2 shows almost a straight line toward greater redistribution since 1947. In 1947, government taxes and benefits reduced the ratio of the aggregate income of the top income quintile to the bottom two income quintiles by around 25 percent. In 1993 the percentage reduction in inequality due to explicit redistribution approached 70 percent.[8] Redistribution, however, did not move in lock-step with pre-redistribution inequality. The upward trend in redistribution is present even prior to the increases in inequality in the 1970s. This suggests that redistribution is not merely an automatic response to increased market inequality but can also occur in the context of steady levels of inequality.

The recent history of redistribution in the United States is instructive and appears to be connected with macro political change. After increasing steadily for four decades, redistribution leveled off during the Reagan administration. The steady increase in redistribution was even reversed for a time during Reagan's second term and George H.W. Bush's time in the White House. Redistribution then reached its highest point under Bill Clinton and was essentially maintained while he remained president.

Figure 4.3 charts the level of inequality in the United States after accounting for the combined impact of market and redistributive mechanisms. This chart shows that while pre-redistribution inequality was remaining steady between 1947 and the early 1970s, increased redistribution pushed post-government levels of inequality markedly lower. In fact, the decline in post-government inequality continued for several years after pre-redistribution inequality began increasing. Even into the late 1970s, post-government inequality was moving lower. Post-government inequality only began to increase during the Reagan era in which explicit redistribution came under attack. During the Reagan and H.W. Bush era, post-government inequality increased and then essentially stagnated at a new higher level during Clinton's presidency.

These pictures provide an interesting story in themselves. The visual evidence seems to argue in favor of the hypotheses of power resources theory regarding the link between politics and income inequality, but

---

[8] Note that the reduction in the T20/B40 ratio is much higher than the reduction in the Gini coefficient discussed in Chapter 2. This is the case because the Gini emphasizes inequality at the middle of the income distribution while the T20/B40 ratio focuses on the top and bottom of the distribution. Since most redistribution is taking from the top quintile and giving to the bottom two quintiles, it makes sense that this measure of redistribution would indicate a higher level of redistribution than when using the Gini.

we can be certain that the paths of distribution and redistribution in the United States are influenced by more than just politics. For example, union membership has been steadily declining at the same time that inequality has risen and redistribution has increased. Of course there are other potential explanations that must be considered as well. This means that rigorous multivariate analysis that takes account of a variety of explanatory factors is needed.

In this chapter and the next, I will analyze two of the three measures discussed above as dependent variables – redistribution and pre-redistribution inequality. These two variables provide the most direct tests of the theoretical predictions of power resources theory. Examining the connection between power resources variables and pre-redistribution inequality provides leverage on the question of whether lower class power resources influence distributional outcomes via market conditioning. If labor union strength and left-party control of government influence pre-redistribution inequality, this would support the conclusion that both market and political power resources influence inequality via a market-conditioning mechanism. The analysis of political power resources and explicit redistribution provides a straightforward test of the distributional impact of power resources via the redistributive mechanism.

Importantly, analyzing these two dependent variables provides direct evidence about the determinants of post-government inequality as well. This is the case because post-government inequality is a direct function of pre-redistribution inequality and redistribution. Redistribution is calculated based on pre-redistribution inequality and post-government inequality [Eq. (4.1)]. From this, post-government inequality can be computed as follows:

$$\text{Post} = \text{Pre}\left(1 - \frac{\text{Redistribution}}{100}\right) \qquad (4.2)$$

An increase in pre-redistribution inequality, by definition, produces an increase in post-government inequality. Contrarily, increases in redistribution decrease post-government inequality. Thus, the effect of an explanatory variable on pre-redistribution inequality or redistribution can be directly translated into an impact on post-government inequality.

Control of the Presidency and Distributional Outcomes

To begin the analysis, I examine the bivariate relationship between party control of the presidency and distributional outcomes. First, I focus on party control and pre-redistribution inequality. Setting aside the effects of market power resources and other potentially confounding factors, I ask whether Democratic presidents are associated with declines in pre-redistribution inequality. Table 4.1 reports the results. Examining the change in pre-redistribution inequality occurring during each 4-year presidential term between 1948 and 2000 shows that the largest 4-year increase in inequality came during Nixon's ill-fated second term. The Democratic presidency of Bill Clinton saw the largest declines in pre-redistribution inequality. On average, the aggregate income ratio of the top quintile to the bottom two quintiles declined by 0.16 during Democratic presidencies and rose by 0.30 under Republican presidents. This result is consistent with power resources theory, but is preliminary given the multitude of other factors that might influence pre-redistribution inequality.

TABLE 4.1. *Change in Pre-Redistribution Inequality by Presidential Administration, 1948–2000*

President	Pre-Redistribution T20/B40 Ratio		
	First Year	Final Year	Change
Truman (D)	2.95	2.95	0
Eisenhower (R)	2.94	2.97	0.03
Eisenhower (R)	2.96	3.37	0.41
Kennedy/Johnson (D)	3.67	3.46	−0.21
Johnson (D)	3.3	3.16	−0.14
Nixon (R)	3.12	3.6	0.48
Nixon/Ford (R)	3.55	4.09	0.54
Carter (D)	4.17	4.43	0.26
Reagan (R)	4.96	5.2	0.24
Reagan (R)	5.2	4.77	−0.43
H.W. Bush (R)	5.11	5.91	0.8
Clinton (D)	6.65	6.11	−0.54
Clinton (D)	5.97	5.64	−0.33
Republican Average			0.30
Democratic Average			−0.16

TABLE 4.2. *Change in Redistribution by Presidential Administration,* *1948–2000*

President	Percent Reduction in Inequality via Redistribution		
	First Year	Final Year	Change
Truman (D)	26.6	28.8	2.2
Eisenhower (R)	29.5	31.7	2.2
Eisenhower (R)	33.8	38.4	4.6
Kennedy/Johnson (D)	40.4	40.2	−0.1
Johnson (D)	38.7	40.5	1.9
Nixon (R)	42.4	47.1	4.7
Nixon/Ford (R)	47.3	55.4	8.0
Carter (D)	55.9	61.6	5.8
Reagan (R)	65.6	64.7	−0.9
Reagan (R)	64.5	60.4	−4.1
H.W. Bush (R)	62.1	68.6	6.5
Clinton (D)	69.6	68.0	−1.6
Clinton (D)	66.2	65.9	−0.3
Republican Average			3.0
Democratic Average			1.31

Table 4.2 reports similar data, but examines government redistribution rather than pre-redistribution inequality. Contrary to expectations, we see that redistribution generally increases more under Republican than Democratic presidential administrations. The evidence on this point, however, is more ambiguous than the evidence on pre-redistribution inequality. While redistribution increased an average of 3 points under Republican presidents and only 1.3 points under Democrats, both the greatest increases and decreases in redistribution occurred during Republican administrations. The Nixon/Ford administration oversaw an 8-point increase in the percent reduction in inequality via government redistribution, which was the largest increase in any administration. The largest decrease in redistribution occurred during Reagan's second term, when redistribution declined by 4.1 points.

The bivariate results for the connection between party control of the presidency and pre-redistribution inequality are consistent with expectations, while the results for redistribution are somewhat puzzling. Both results certainly deserve more detailed multivariate analysis, but the redistribution results merit some further discussion at this point. It is interesting to note that the largest increases in redistribution occurred during the same period that pre-redistribution inequality increased most rapidly. This is consistent with the welfare economics theory of Meltzer and Richard (1981) which predicts that higher levels of inequality will produce greater demand for redistribution. This is also consistent with the operation of certain social welfare programs designed as a social insurance safety net. If economic factors that produce high levels of pre-redistribution inequality also produce conditions that place more individuals on the public dole, we would expect to see an increase in redistribution accompany an increase in pre-redistribution inequality regardless of which party controls the government because under existing policies more redistribution will occur naturally.

If such a relationship exists, it presents a catch-22 of sorts for parties seeking to influence distributional outcomes. Recalling the two mechanisms through which party control might influence overall distributional outcomes – the market and the state – it could be counterproductive to utilize both mechanisms in tandem. If the powers of government are used to condition market outcomes in a way that produces greater pre-redistribution equality, these gains may be canceled out by corresponding reductions in redistribution. Similar challenges would face those with inegalitarian goals. In order to substantively influence overall distributional outcomes (post-government inequality), policies that avoid this catch-22 are necessary. The trick is to create redistributive policies that are not driven completely by pre-redistribution inequality. To learn whether market and political power resources achieve real influence on distributional outcomes, more fully specified models must be developed. That is the task to which I now turn.

A Multivariate Analysis of Lower Class Power Resources and Distributional Outcomes

I conduct a multivariate analysis of two dependent variables: redistribution, the percent by which government programs decrease inequality, and pre-redistribution inequality, the distribution of income prior to the effect of taxes and transfers. Indicators of market and political

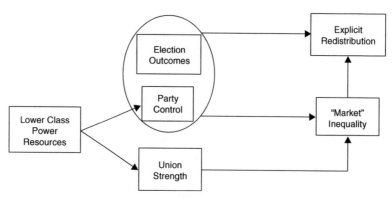

FIGURE 4.4. Power Resources Portion of the Model

power resources will be of most central theoretical interest in both analyses. In this chapter I utilize three standard indicators of political power resources – Democratic control of the presidency, Democratic share of seats in the House of Representatives, and Democratic share of seats in the Senate. I use union membership as an indicator of market power resources. This analysis is rooted in the overarching theoretical model first discussed in Chapter 1 and depicted in Figure 1.8. The focus here is on the aspects of the model that build directly on a classic conception of power resources theory. The specific portion of the model examined in this chapter is shown in Figure 4.4.

In addition to these classic power resources variables, I also give attention to variables associated with rival theories, most particularly the logic of industrialism thesis, but also the state-centric theory. Concepts associated with the logic of industrialism thesis include deindustrialization, economic conditions, and the size and composition of the labor force. More specifically, I use the following measures to capture these concepts: the percent of the labor force in nonmanufacturing jobs, the unemployment rate, the percent of the population over age 65, the female labor force participation rate, and the percent of the population with at least a high school education. In some parts of the analysis, I include two further measures that have been discussed in the existing literature on income inequality in the United States (Danziger and Gottschalk 1995) and could be tied loosely to the logic of industrialism thesis, but have not generally been discussed in this theoretical context – the percent of households headed by single females and the percent of the population composed of new immigrants. The state-centric theory emphasizes state structure as an explanation for state activity. Measures of constitutional structure are often associated with this theory, but clearly in a period in which no major constitutional structures were changed in the United States, this theory is likely less central. However, I incorporate divided government in my analysis to account for the fact that the United States has a system of separation of powers.[9]

A Brief Methodological Digression: Error Correction Models for Time Series Analysis

I utilize error correction models (ECMs) to estimate the connection between indicators of lower class power resources and both pre-redistribution inequality and redistribution (Banerjee et al. 1993, Davidson et al. 1978). Given the relatively recent introduction of these models to political science, a few explanatory details about these time series models are necessary. ECMs are appropriate when theory suggests a dependent variable responds to short-term changes in independent variables and/or maintains a long-term level consistent with these variables. This is consistent with the situation in this analysis because when a shift in partisan control or union strength occurs, there can be an immediate impact, but additional effects could also be distributed over time such that the full effect is not fully felt immediately. I hypothesize that pre-redistribution inequality and redistribution are responsive to changes in lower class power resources. However, even if shifts in power resources do not quickly produce different distributional outcomes, inequality should gradually decrease if high levels of lower class power resources are maintained.

More specifically, I estimate the short- and long-term effects of power resources using the single equation method for estimating ECMs. This strategy is selected in favor of the most common alternative, the Engle and Granger (1987) two-step estimator, for two reasons. First, unlike the two-step method the single equation model

---

[9] None of the models are reported because they produced no significant results and did not fundamentally alter the substantive results reported. Reporting these results would have complicated the tables dramatically since interactions between party control and divided government were included in these models. The additional results did not justify the added complexity of the tables.

does not impose the assumption of cointegration on the series analyzed (De Boef and Keele 2008). In fact, the single equation ECM is a modified version of an autoregressive distributed lag model in which the dependent variable is a function of its past values and past values of the independent variables. This means that the single equation ECM can be applied to both integrated and stationary series (Banerjee et al. 1993, De Boef 2001, De Boef and Granato 1999, De Boef and Keele 2008). Second, the single equation estimator is preferred in small samples (Banerjee 1986, De Boef and Granato 1999). Overall, use of the single equation model can be justified in a broader range of circumstances than the two-step method.[10]

One way to express a bivariate single-equation error correction model is as follows:

$$\Delta Y_t = \beta_1 \Delta X_{t-i} - \beta_2 (Y_{t-1} - \beta_3 X_{t-1} - \lambda) + \epsilon_t \qquad (4.3)$$

In words, this equation simply tells us that changes in a dependent variable Y are determined by short-term changes in an independent variable X as well as divergence from a long run equilibrium between X and Y. Imagine, for example, that a change in short-term interest rates is connected to long-term interest rates by an error correction mechanism. Long run rates might rise in response to a change in short-run rates (with the value of i determining the lag before the onset of this "short-term" effect). But that may not be the only connection between the variables. It is also possible (in fact more likely based on empirical analysis) that short and long rates maintain an equilibrium relationship such that disturbing short-term rates creates a situation in which long-term rates are too low relative to short-term rates. Over time,

---

[10] ECMs are also a way to correct for any problems of nonstationarity in a dependent variable. If a dependent variable has a deterministic trend such as increasing consistently over time or contains a data generating process that produces some other form of nonstationarity, statistically significant results can be spurious and lead to incorrect inferences. This is obviously a situation to be avoided. The classic solution for a nonstationary dependent variable is to analyze the first difference, or change, in the dependent variable. In an ECM, change in the dependent variable is analyzed, so nonstationarity is generally not a problem. However, it is theoretically possible though extremely rare for a differenced dependent variable to be nonstationary. To guard against this situation I tested all of my differenced dependent variables for stationarity. Multiple tests (including Dickey-Fuller, Phillips-Perron, and Kwiatkowski, Phillips, Schmidt, and Shin) confirm that analyzing change in redistribution and change in pre-redistribution inequality satisfies the stationarity requirement.

this deviation (error) from the long run equilibrium will be eliminated (corrected) by an increase in long-term rates. An ECM takes account of both possible mechanisms. The first type of connection is captured by the effect of changes in short-term rates on changes in long-term rates. The second type of connection is captured by examining the lagged distance between short- and long-term rates in levels.

In the analysis below, I utilize the following transformed version of equation (4.3) to estimate ECMs:

$$\Delta Y_t = \alpha_0 + \alpha_1 Y_{t-1} + \beta_1 \Delta X_{t-i} + \beta_2 X_{t-1} + \epsilon_t \tag{4.4}$$

For each independent variable X, then, we have up to two parameter estimates – β_1 for the differenced variable, its change from one point in time to the next, and β_2 for the lagged level of the variable.[11] But what do these two parameter estimates mean? In this simple bivariate example, β_1 provides an estimate of the initial change in the dependent variable produced in the short term by a shock to the independent variable.[12] For example, if public opinion shifts in a liberal direction and policymaking responds by shifting in the same direction, the short-term coefficient, β_1, provides an estimate of the size of this shift. To explain some terminology that will be used extensively in the remainder of the book, then, this is the type of effect that will be referred to as the "short-term" effect. This does not mean that the effect is impermanent, but simply that the effect happens all at once at a specified point in time.

β_2 provides a portion of the information needed to estimate the "long-term" impact, which is slightly more complicated to explain. This is also called the error correction component of the model. The long-term impact is the portion of the connection between X and Y that does not occur at a particular point in time but is distributed temporally such that a portion of the impact is felt in each period over a time span. Returning to a substantive example, if the impact of public opinion is

---

[11] The lagged level can be dropped from the equation if we find that it has no statistically significant impact.

[12] The onset of this initial impact could be contemporaneous, with a shift in the independent variable at time t creating a shift in the dependent variable at time t. It could also be lagged, such that the initial shift in the dependent variable may not occur for some specified number of time periods; thus the $t - i$ subscript on the ΔX parameter.

linked to policymaking via an error correction mechanism, a shock to public opinion disturbs the long run equilibrium between opinion and policy, and this divergence from the equilibrium will eventually be corrected over time. The size of this long run impact is a function not only of β_2 but also of α_1, which is known as the error correction rate. The full long-term impact of a shock to X on Y via the error correction component, known as the long run multiplier, is computed by dividing β_2 by α_1.

Aside from being a component in the computation of the impact (via the error correction mechanism) of the independent variable on the dependent variable, the error correction rate (α_1) also tells us something about how quickly a disturbance from the long run equilibrium is eliminated. Estimates of α_1 will in practice be between 0.0 and -1.0 in appropriately specified ECMs, and the closer this parameter is to -1.0, the more quickly errors are corrected. The substantive interpretation of the coefficient is the proportion of the disturbance from equilibrium that will be corrected in each time period, beginning at $t + 1$. From this error correction rate, we can then make inferences about how quickly the total long run impact is felt.

I will often utilize terminology from the ECM tradition to describe the results. "Short-term" effects refer to the initial impact of X on Y. "Long-term effects," "effects via the error correction mechanism," and "the long run multiplier" all refer to the effect of X on Y that is distributed over time. Finally, "total effects" refer to a combination of short- and long-term effects. I turn now to the heart of the analysis.

Analyzing Redistribution

I begin by examining the determinants of the redistributive impact of government, which is the classic dependent variable in the power resources theory tradition. Redistribution, as defined above, is measured as the percentage reduction in the ratio of the income of the top income quintile to the income of the bottom two quintiles that is attributable to government taxes and benefits. Table 4.3 reports the results of two ECM models of government redistribution. In each of these models, the variables most central to testing power resources theory are the indicators of political power resources. The expectation is that Democratic Party control of government should

TABLE 4.3. *Explaining Government Redistribution, 1947–2000*

Independent Variables	Δ Redistribution	
	(1)	(2)
Error Correction Rate	−0.30**	−0.37***
	(0.13)	(0.12)
Political Power Resources		
Δ Democratic President$_{t-1}$	0.54	0.02
	(0.74)	(0.72)
Democratic President$_{t-1}$	1.10*	1.17**
	(0.57)	(0.48)
Δ % Senate Democrat$_{t-1}$	0.01	
	(0.07)	
% Senate Democrat$_{t-1}$	−0.09	
	(0.06)	
Δ % House Democrat$_{t-1}$	0.08	
	(0.06)	
% House Democrat$_{t-1}$	0.04	
	(0.07)	
Labor Market Factors		
Δ % Unemployed$_t$	1.64***	0.66***
	(0.55)	(0.23)
% Unemployed$_{t-1}$	0.62*	0.56*
	(0.35)	(0.31)
Δ % Nonmanufacturing$_t$	−1.06	
	(0.66)	
% Nonmanufacturing$_{t-1}$	−0.10	
	(0.29)	
Demographic Factors		
Δ % Aged 65+$_t$	−0.36	7.52*
	(5.75)	(3.85)
% Aged 65+$_{t-1}$	3.71***	2.99***
	(1.20)	(0.96)
Δ % New Immigrants$_t$	−0.58	
	(1.24)	
% New Immigrants$_{t-1}$	−1.85	
	(1.21)	
Response to Inequality		
Δ Pre-Redist. Inequality$_t$	4.57***	5.04***
	(0.87)	(0.77)
Pre-Redist. Inequality$_{t-1}$	−1.14	
	(0.99)	
Constant	−12.69	−17.02***
	(17.27)	(5.98)
Adj. R^2	0.79	0.77
N	52	52

Two-tailed significance levels: *$p \leq 0.10$; **$p \leq 0.05$; ***$p \leq 0.01$.

Note: Table entries are time series regression coefficients representing a single-equation error correction model with standard errors in parentheses.

increase the equalizing influence of government. I begin with an over-specified model of redistribution to provide a rigorous test of power resources theory versus alternative explanations and then proceed to a reduced form model that presents the most parsimonious model of redistribution.

Model 1 represents the most fully specified model. In addition to Democratic control of the presidency and shares of Democratic seats in the Senate and in the House, I include a variety of variables that are related to the logic of industrialism hypothesis. I organize these variables into two further categories: labor market factors (unemployment and deindustrialization) and demographic factors (population aged 65 and over and immigration). Unemployment should increase redistribution because increases in unemployment will automatically generate unemployment insurance payments. Deindustrialization might have a similar impact, as manufacturing workers are displaced and need retraining to obtain new employment. The size of the elderly population should also increase redistribution given the importance and magnitude of programs targeted toward this constituency such as Medicare and Social Security. McCarty et al. (2006) argue that immigration should influence redistributive policy. In addition to these variables that are related to the logic of industrialism thesis, I include a control for pre-redistribution inequality with the idea that higher levels of inequality will generate greater redistribution because of formulaic policies activated by the same conditions that generate high levels of pre-redistribution inequality.

The results for Model 1 support the predictions of power resources theory as well as some of the predictions of the logic of industrialism. First and foremost, the coefficients reported at the top of the table show that Democratic control of the presidency increases redistribution in the long term. Also as expected, the unemployment rate, the elderly population, and pre-redistribution inequality increase government redistribution. However, we observe no significant impact of partisan strength in Congress on redistribution in either the short or long term, and the same can be said for deindustrialization and immigration.[13] Model 1, then, is over-specified.

---

[13] These results would be even more supportive of power resources theory if partisanship of both the presidency and Congress influenced explicit redistribution. As it

A more restricted model is reported in the next column. Deindustrialization and partisan strength in Congress, along with the estimate of the nonsignificant long-term impact of pre-redistribution inequality, are dropped from the earlier model to produce a more parsimonious and efficiently specified model of redistribution. This model includes just four explanatory variables – Democratic control of the presidency, the unemployment rate, the elderly population, and pre-redistribution inequality. The model estimated is as follows, dropping insignificant coefficients for the sake of simplicity:

$$\Delta\text{Redist}_t = -17.02 + .66\Delta\text{Unemp}_t + 7.52\Delta\text{Elderly}_t + 5.04\Delta\text{Pre}_t$$

$$- .37\text{Redist}_{t-1} + 1.17\text{DemPres}_{t-1} + .56\text{Unemp}_{t-1}$$

$$+ 2.98\text{Elderly}_{t-1} + \epsilon_t \qquad (4.5)$$

As in the first model, Democratic control of the presidency produces a long-term increase in redistribution. This supports the central prediction of power resources theory. The two coefficients estimated for Democratic president and the estimate of the error correction rate,

---

stands, only the presidency matters, and this result is repeated in the later analysis of pre-redistribution inequality. While the fact that the proportion of seats held by Democrats in the House and the Senate does not directly influence distributional outcomes is not supportive of power resources theory, neither do the insignificant results disprove power resources theory. It is still somewhat puzzling why no effect can be found for left party strength in Congress. In fact, I have tried a variety of specifications and measurement strategies to account for Democratic presence in the legislative branch. I included dichotomous variables for party control of the House, the Senate, and Congress as a whole. I have even diverged from a direct measure of partisanship to examine ideological common space scores. I have also utilized strategies that account for the super-majoritarian nature of the Senate and the role of divided government. Regardless of the strategy, no significant results can be found for the legislative branch. It may be the case that I have overlooked a method of modeling the partisan composition of Congress. It might also be that the president has such a degree of agenda control that it is actually correct to conclude that only the partisanship of the president matters directly for determining distributional outcomes. However, we will see in the next chapter that macro policy influences distributional outcomes. Since the partisan composition of Congress has been previously shown to influence macro policy (Erikson et al. 2002), it would be inappropriate to conclude that Congress has no role in shaping distributional outcomes. I do not explore the underlying reasons for this null result because such an exploration is more relevant to theories of policy making than to power resources theory, which is my primary focus here. This remains an interesting question that might be worthy of future exploration in a different theoretical context.

which is 37 percent annually, give us a great deal of substantive information. When a Democratic president is elected, this shift in party control does not have an immediate impact. However, over the course of time, the shift to a Democratic president increases redistribution by 3.16 points. More tangibly, if government is already reducing inequality through redistribution by 23 percent, when a Democrat takes over the presidency from a Republican, government reduction of inequality will increase to more than 26 percent over the course of about 8 years. This is a substantial impact given that redistribution changes on average each year by less than 2 points.

While the total effect of Democratic control of the presidency is a 3.16 point increase in redistribution, it is important to remember that this impact is distributed over time, such that only 37 percent of the disequilibrium is corrected each year, beginning the year after control of the presidency changes. Thus, the first year after a Democratic takeover (year two of an administration), the model predicts a 1.17 point increase in redistribution. After this impact, a 1.99 point disequilibrium remains, 37 percent of which, or 0.74 points, is corrected in the second year after a Democratic takeover of the White House. Continuing this pattern, redistribution increases 0.46 points in the third year after Democratic control occurs. Thus, over the course of a first presidential administration, the effect of Democratic as opposed to Republican control totals a 2.37 point increase in redistribution. The total effect of two consecutive Democratic administrations is a 3.09 point increase. This effectively tells us that 75 percent of the total impact of a shift in presidential control occurs during the first term of a president, while nearly 98 percent of the total impact is felt over the course of two administrations. These results also indicate that maintaining a shift in party control for a third presidential term would have little additional impact on government redistribution, at least through the direct mechanism analyzed here. Democratic control for a third presidential term would, of course, maintain the same level of redistribution, while switching to Republican control would result in a decline in the level of redistribution.

The results reported in the table focus on variables related to power resources theory and the logic of industrialism thesis. I also entertained models including variables related to state-centric theories of welfare state activity. State-centric theories focus on institutional characteristics of government organization in explaining welfare state development. Given my focus on one country over time, during a period in which institutional structures remained essentially constant at the national level, meaningful state-centric variables are few. I did, however, consider divided government as a way to tap the effect of the separation of powers institutional arrangement of the United States. In addition to the variables included in Model 2 of Table 4.3, I added an indicator of divided government, as well as an interaction term of divided government and Democratic control of the presidency. The goal here was to determine whether the substantive impact of party control of the presidency is augmented during times of unified government. Adding dividing government and the interaction term added no explanatory power to the model, and none of the additional variables were significant. Thus, these results fail to lead to any additional insights, other than to say that there is no support for the conclusion that the impact of political power resources are conditioned by divided or unified government. This may not be surprising given the limited impact of party strength in Congress in the earlier models.

Analyzing Pre-Redistribution Inequality

In the analysis above, I addressed the question of whether political power resources influenced the path of government redistribution in the post–World War II United States. The answer is a resounding yes. These results show that the most fundamental prediction of power resources theory applies in the context of the United States, and the findings are broadly consistent with similar analyses conducted using shorter time periods and different indicators of welfare state effort (Hibbs and Dennis 1988, Kelly 2004). Now, I turn to an analysis of a more novel implication of power resources theory – that both market *and* political power resources influence pre-redistribution inequality. This analysis addresses the question of whether state activity influences income inequality through market conditioning in addition to the more traditional mechanism of explicit redistribution.

Table 4.4 reports the results of five error correction models of pre-redistribution inequality.[14] In this analysis, I present four preliminary

---

[14] It is possible that distributional outcomes such as pre-redistribution inequality influence lower class mobilization that translate into the indicators of power resources

TABLE 4.4. *Explaining Pre-Redistribution Inequality, 1947–2000*

Independent Variables	Δ Pre-Redistribution Inequality				
	(1)	(2)	(3)	(4)	(5)
Error Correction Rate	−0.39*** (0.14)	−0.81*** (0.16)	−0.52*** (0.14)	−0.76*** (0.13)	−0.74*** (0.13)
Political Power Resources					
Δ Democratic President$_{t-1}$	−0.27* (0.14)	−0.34*** (0.12)	−0.23* (0.12)	−0.28*** (0.09)	−0.30*** (0.09)
Democratic President$_{t-1}$	−0.07 (0.10)	0.07 (0.09)	0.01 (0.09)		
Δ % Senate Democrat$_{t-1}$	−0.02 (0.02)				
% Senate Democrat$_{t-1}$	−0.00 (0.01)				
Δ % House Democrat$_{t-1}$	0.01 (0.01)				
% House Democrat$_{t-1}$	0.00 (0.01)				
Market Power Resources					
Δ % Unionized$_{t-1}$	0.03 (0.08)	0.01 (0.07)	0.01 (0.07)	0.02 (0.06)	0.02 (0.06)
% Unionized$_{t-1}$	−0.06*** (0.02)	−0.08** (0.04)	−0.05* (0.03)	−0.10*** (0.02)	−0.09*** (0.02)
Labor Market Factors					
Δ % Unemployed$_{t-1}$		0.19** (0.09)		0.10 (0.08)	0.05 (0.03)
% Unemployed$_{t-1}$		0.10* (0.05)		0.11*** (0.03)	0.10*** (0.03)

Δ %Nonmanufacturing$_{t-1}$		−0.20*		−0.07	
		(0.11)		(0.10)	
% Nonmanufacturing$_{t-1}$		0.07			
		(0.06)			
Δ Female Labor Part$_{t-1}$		−0.04			
		(0.11)			
Female Labor Part$_{t-1}$		0.00			
		(0.02)			
Demographic Factors					
Δ % Aged 65+$_{t-1}$			0.97		
			(0.87)		
% Aged 65+$_{t-1}$			−0.27		
			(0.27)		
Δ % New Immigrants$_{t-1}$			−0.84***	−0.70***	−0.73***
			(0.25)	(0.21)	(0.20)
% New Immigrants$_{t-1}$			0.64***	0.41**	0.46***
			(0.22)	(0.19)	(0.17)
Δ % SF Headed HH$_{t-1}$			−0.10		
			(0.14)		
% SF Headed HH$_{t-1}$			0.11		
			(0.08)		
Constant	3.25***	−0.34	3.39*	4.94***	4.67***
	(1.09)	(4.83)	(1.90)	(1.01)	(0.93)
Adj. R^2	0.22	0.45	0.33	0.56	0.57
N	52	52	52	52	52

Two-tailed significance levels: *$p \leq 0.10$; **$p \leq 0.05$; ***$p \leq 0.01$.
Note: Table reports time series regression coefficients representing a single-equation error correction model with standard errors in parentheses.

models that include subsets of explanatory factors to assess the sensitivity of the effect of the primary theoretical variables to specification. The indicators of market and political power resources are included in every model.

Model 1 examines the impact of market and political power resources on pre-redistribution inequality in isolation from other potential explanatory factors. In a nutshell, both market power resources, in the form of union membership, and political power resources, in the form of Democratic control of the presidency, influence pre-redistribution inequality. Democratic strength in the Congress, however, has no discernible impact, so these variables are dropped from the remaining models. It is worthy to note that a wide variety of measurement strategies for Congressional party strength were employed, from simple party control of the House and the Senate to measures that accounted for the super-majoritarian nature of policymaking in the Senate, and all produced identical results.[15]

Model 2 considers three measures of labor market characteristics – unemployment, deindustrialization, and female labor force participation – in addition to the statistically significant indicators of market and political power resources included in Model 1. Unemployment and deindustrialization were also considered as explanations of redistribution in the earlier analysis, but female labor force participation is a variable that has received greater attention in studies attempting to explain income inequality as opposed to government redistribution. Thus, I also consider it here alongside the other labor market factors. In this model both market and political power resources remain important determinants of pre-redistribution inequality. In addition to the power resources variables, unemployment and deindustrialization also have a statistically significant impact on pre-redistribution inequality. Thus, these variables will be included in the final model, but for deindustrialization only the immediate impact will be considered since Model 2 shows that this variable has no additional long-term impact that is

theory. This could create simultaneity bias in the models that I estimate. To guard against this I lag the impact of change in power resources variables on change in distributional outcomes. It is not likely that changes in power resources this year are influenced by changes in distributional outcomes next year.

[15] See footnote 13 for a discussion of this null result.

phased in over time (as evidenced by the insignificant coefficient for lagged levels of nonmanufacturing jobs).

Model 3 removes labor market factors and considers three demographic factors that have been suggested as determinants of income inequality – the elderly population, immigration, and single-female headed households. Each of these factors is expected to increase inequality. Of these variables, immigration is the only factor that influences pre-redistribution inequality. Interestingly, the short- and long-term impact of immigration work against each other. While the initial impact of an increase in immigration is a decline in inequality, this decline is eventually canceled out and, in fact, reversed over time. The short-term, negative impact is -0.84, while the total long-term impact is $0.64/0.52 = 1.21$. The immediate and long-term impact of immigration are carried into Model 4.

Model 4 simply puts the previous three models together to provide an assessment of pre-redistribution inequality that considers political power resources, market power resources, labor market factors, and demographic factors in a single model. When considered jointly, the main results of theoretical interest remain, but deindustrialization loses its explanatory significance in this model. These first four models show that the impact of lower class power resources is robust. Regardless of which economic and demographic controls are included in the model, the impact of party control of the White House and union strength on inequality is consistent. Model 5 presents a final analysis of pre-redistribution inequality, which represents the most parsimonious model.

This final model produces results that are consistent with power resources theory. First, we see that union membership has a negative impact on pre-redistribution inequality. This provides support for a classic power resources theory prediction. Second, and even more importantly, this model shows that political power resources in the form of Democratic control of the presidency also influence pre-redistribution inequality. This supports the conclusion that state activity influences distributional outcomes via market conditioning in addition to the more traditionally conceptualized mechanism of explicit redistribution. Democratic control of the presidency increases explicit redistribution, but also decreases pre-redistribution inequality.

Explicit redistribution and market conditioning are two distinct mechanisms for distributional impact that are used in tandem to influence the path of income inequality in the United States. Interestingly, the impact of party control on pre-redistribution inequality is immediate, while the impact on redistribution is distributed over time. When a Republican takes over the White House, this analysis shows that pre-redistribution inequality will increase by 0.30 points *in the year after party control changes*. This is a large impact given that pre-redistribution inequality only goes up or down by an average of 0.22 points each year. However, it takes two full presidential terms for the total impact of party control on redistribution to be observed. This seems to indicate, at least with regard to the direct effect of party control on distributional outcomes, that changes in redistribution are politically difficult to generate, while conditioning market outcomes can be achieved more directly, easily, and quickly.

Other than power resources explanations, only the rate of unemployment and immigration have a statistically significant impact on pre-redistribution inequality in the fully specified model. In this case the impact of unemployment is substantively powerful in only its long-term impact. A 1 percent increase in unemployment increases pre-redistribution inequality by less than half the amount produced by a shift from Democratic to Republican control of the presidency. As mentioned earlier, the short- and long-term impact of immigration work against each other. An increase in immigration leads to an initial increase in inequality that is essentially erased by later increases in inequality over the long term. Finally, as with explicit redistribution, in models not shown, I considered divided government and its interaction with party control as potential explanatory factors. No results of interest were produced. Either divided government is not consequential or the data analyzed here are simply not of high enough quality to produce confirmation of the importance of the separation of powers.

CONCLUSION

The most important message of this chapter is that power resources theory can be effectively applied in the context of the United States. Despite several factors that make the United States a challenging context in which to analyze power resources theory, its central predictions hold true. Market power resources in the form of union membership drive down the level of inequality produced within the market. Political power resources influence the amount of redistribution generated by the state, with the direct effect of Democratic strength being an increase in redistribution.

I went beyond these two traditional predictions of power resources theory, however, and the analysis produced some surprising results. Specifically, I hypothesized that political power resources would be used to influence market action as well as government activity. Rooted in my discussion of market conditioning as a mechanism of distributional impact in Chapter 2, it seems reasonable to suspect that control of the state by lower class interests would produce an equalizing impact via both market conditioning and explicit redistribution. I tested this hypothesis by examining the connection between indicators of lower class power resources and inequality measured prior to the effects of government taxes and benefits. The results lead to the conclusion that party control of government matters for both redistribution and government conditioned market inequality, meaning that market conditioning and redistribution are tools of state distributional impact. *Even before redistribution occurs, government matters.*

The primary political variables of interest in this chapter were the relative strength of the two major parties in government. Clearly, partisan dynamics matter, and such an emphasis on party control is closely connected to previous studies in the power resources tradition. The reason power resources theory suggests that party control should matter for distributional outcomes, of course, is that different parties will pursue different policies. Policies, however, are rarely assessed directly in cross-national studies of power resources theory. Assessing policy is important because the U.S. parties do not always consistently support or oppose redistribution and reductions in inequality. Bill Clinton, for example, was a Democrat who supported welfare reform measures that made it harder for the poor to remain on the welfare rolls. This was not a classic redistributional stance by a Democrat. In the next chapter, I account for such policy variation by focusing explicitly on the ideological tone of policy as a more proximate cause of distributional outcomes than partisanship. In doing so, I bring a major theory from comparative politics into direct communication with the macro politics model of U.S. politics.

5

Macro Policy and Distributional Processes

The theoretical focus of the previous chapter was on power resources. There we saw that the fundamental predictions of power resources theory for distributional outcomes are borne out in the United States. Market and political power resources, as traditionally measured, have an impact on income inequality. Labor union strength influences income inequality measured prior to government redistribution. Left party control produces lower levels of inequality through both market conditioning and explicit redistribution. In this chapter, I shift the emphasis from power resources theory, an idea originating in the comparative study of welfare states, to the macro politics model, which has its roots in studies of American politics.

As discussed in Chapter 1, the macro politics model examines relationships between parts of the U.S. governing system, such as public opinion, presidential approval, partisanship, elections, and public policy at the aggregate level. The argument is that the parts of the system behave predictably and orderly. Citizens express preferences about competing policy alternatives, the preferred alternatives are enacted, and citizens then judge the quality of the outcomes produced. Tests of this model show that liberal shifts in public opinion produce liberal shifts in policy because policymakers respond to changes in public opinion and, if they do not, they are replaced through popular elections.

Aggregate public opinion influences the course of public policy in the United States, and this previous finding is an important underpinning of my work. But the macro politics model in essence assumes that changes in public policy produce changes in societal outcomes (though see Kellstedt et al. 1993). Based on the discussion in Chapter 3, it should be clear that in the realm of income inequality, shifts to the left in public policy are expected to produce reductions in income inequality. However, this implication of the macro politics model has not been rigorously tested (Figure 1.6). If citizens exert influence over public policy but policy does not influence important societal outcomes, the substantive impact of the opinion-policy link declines. My goal in this chapter is to determine whether the ideological content of policy, rather than partisan control, systematically influences distributional outcomes.

MICRO AND MACRO: THE LOGIC OF MACRO POLITICS

At its heart, the macro politics model is about how the governing system of the United States functions. Ideally, a democratic system would be composed of highly informed and active citizens who influence the behavior of policymakers and hold them accountable for their actions. Decades of individual-level survey research, however, have shown that the ideal citizen at the heart of this picture is a rare bird. The empirical debunking of the democratic ideal in American politics is rooted in the individual voting behavior tradition. Beginning with the Columbia studies of the 1940s and continuing with the publication of *The American Voter* (Campbell et al. 1960), a venerated line of research in political science has raised a variety of problems regarding the translation of citizen preferences into public policy. The problem is that individual citizens in the United States are not particularly informed about contemporary policy issues, do not appear to care all that much about who wins election contests, and do not organize their political ideas around an ideology in ways that facilitate the communication of policy preferences through voting at the polls. Since elections are the only formal mechanism for control of public policy by citizens, these consistently confirmed findings about the individual voter in the United States are troubling.

A new and different research paradigm in political science began to take shape in the late 1980s (Erikson et al. 2002, Page and Shapiro 1992, Stimson 1999, Stimson et al. 1995, Wlezien 1995).

This new research moved the emphasis from the micro-level individual voter to the macro-level citizenry as a collective. Research in this macro tradition, though not questioning the view of the individual voter developed in the previous four decades, does raise problems with the system-level conclusions that micro studies suggest. The micro tradition essentially concludes that meaningful democratic control of public policy is impossible, but the macro tradition questions whether the aggregation of mostly uninformed, uninterested, and nonideological voters produces an uninformed, uninterested, and nonideological electorate. According to macro analysis, the problem with drawing inferences about the political system based on the typical voter described in micro analyses is the surprising finding that atypically informed citizens drive the overall tendency of aggregate public opinion.

The theoretical argument of the macro paradigm is as follows. Democracy has both an individual and a collective component. Democratic theory in part calls on government to be responsive to the preferences of individual citizens, but the translation of *collective* preferences into collective outcomes is more central to democracy. Research at the individual level clearly shows that most people are not enlightened in the sense of caring deeply about political issues and of fitting preferences in one arena together with preferences in another. In other words, individual preferences are noisy and contain a minimal, if any, policy signal. However, one must be mindful of the fact that government responsiveness to citizen preferences is an aggregate phenomenon, and it is important to note that there are some citizens who go against the norm, having large amounts of political interest and information and adopting their political preferences around logical ideologies.

When uninformed citizens change their preferences, they do so in an essentially random way because there is no underlying organizational principle for these citizens' opinions. Highly informed and ideologically oriented citizens, on the other hand, make predictable and consistent changes in their issue preferences across a variety of policy domains. Therefore, any change in aggregate public opinion that is observed from one time to the next cannot be driven by uninformed citizens because their opinion changes are random, with one person's random change canceling out another's random change. Instead, aggregate opinion change is driven by the highly informed who transmit less error-laden opinions and, thus, carries a meaningful policy signal (the public mood) that can be communicated through elections. This is why aggregate preferences on a wide array of domestic policy issues in the United States move together over time in orderly and predictable ways despite the true finding that most individual citizens do not possess orderly and predictable preferences.[1]

In sum, quantitative analyses of the individual voter in the United States debunked democratic theory's view of the enlightened citizen, but the new conceptualization and measurement of public opinion developed in the macro paradigm rescued democratic theory's view of the enlightened citizenry. The macro conception of public opinion forcefully demonstrates that it is theoretically possible for the U.S. electorate to send meaningful policy messages to government officials. At the aggregate level, public opinion sends an ideologically directed signal about preferred public policies. When attitudes on one political issue move toward the ideological left, attitudes on other issues generally follow a similar path (Stimson 1999).

The macro politics model does not stop by demonstrating that aggregate public opinion projects ideological preferences, but builds on this fundamental finding by assessing the impact of the public mood on policymaking. The question is whether the ideological content of public opinion influences the ideological direction of public policy (Erikson et al. 2002, Stimson et al. 1995). Using policymaking data from all three constitutional branches of government, research in the macro politics tradition shows that when public opinion shifts to the left, public policy responds in the same direction. For the elected branches of government, this popular influence over policymaking occurs through two paths. First, elections provide an opportunity for the citizenry to place like-minded representatives in charge of government. Second, because of the re-election motive of elected officials, public policy responds to shifts in public opinion between elections. Interestingly, there is evidence that the decisions of the unelected judicial branch, likely because of its need to maintain legitimacy with the mass public and elected

---

[1] Enns and Kellstedt (2008) tell a theoretically different story that leads to the same fundamental conclusion. They show that people at all levels of political sophistication receive information and change their opinions in similar ways. Under this conception of macro opinion change, aggregate opinion is perhaps even more meaningful.

officials, is responsive to public opinion (Erikson et al. 2002, McGuire and Stimson 2004, Stimson et al. 1995).

Research in the macro politics tradition demonstrates that, at the aggregate level, changes in public opinion produce changes in public policy. This evidence is used to support the conclusion that the U.S. governing system provides a large measure of democratic control over the government – that the U.S. governing system fosters democratic representation. While this is probably a correct conclusion, it is important to remember that democratic control of government is normatively important largely because of the influence and power that government wields over society. So, democratic theory is really about more than determining the policies that government enacts. It is also about the influence that government has on society through these policies. Ideally, it is this influence on society that citizens are able to control through public policy.

While it may be true that aggregate public opinion influences the course of public policy in the United States, the macro politics model leaves the question of whether or not changes in public policy produce changes in societal outcomes largely untested. In the realm of income inequality, a leftward shift in policy should produce quite different distributional consequences than a move to the right according to the macro politics model. If citizens exert influence over public policy, but public policy does not influence important societal outcomes, then the importance of the representation for which the macro politics model finds support is minimized. It is wonderful that citizens influence public policy, but this fact matters little if public policy does not exert systematic influence on societal outcomes over which there is political contestation. I extend the macro politics model by examining whether income inequality in the United States has been systematically and predictably influenced by the ideological direction of public policy during the post-World War II era.

MACRO POLITICS, POWER RESOURCES, AND THE DISTRIBUTIONAL CONSEQUENCES OF POLICY

While the theoretical emphasis in this chapter is the macro politics model rather than power resources theory, these theories need not be viewed in isolation from one another – the analysis of this chapter, in fact, builds directly on the previous chapter. The macro politics model is broad in its scope of analysis, examining as many aspects of the American governing system as possible. Power resources theory, on the other hand, is focused on class conflict and distributional outcomes. Despite these differences, I combine the two theories to provide a more complete picture of distributional processes. Left party control is a central indicator of lower class power resources in power resources theory, and this was the key explanatory concept in the previous chapter's analysis. But election outcomes, as a path that connects public opinion and policy outputs, are also an important component of the macro politics model. The macro politics model speaks of "election outcomes" and power resources theory discusses "party control of government." As Figure 1.8 depicted, these are identical concepts that create a direct overlap between the macro politics model and power resources theory.

Chapter 4, in part, presented a straightforward test of two central predictions of power resources theory – that left party control of government will produce greater government redistribution and will also lower overall levels of income inequality. This fundamental expectation was supported by the analysis. The evidence presented in the previous chapter can also be interpreted as supportive of the macro politics model. Party control of the policymaking institutions of government, produced by election outcomes, is one part of the macro politics model. Showing that Democratic control of the presidency produces more redistribution and less inequality is certainly consistent with the macro politics model. But in the macro politics model, election outcomes are merely a precursor to the ultimate outcome of the political system – public policy (Erikson et al. 2002). Thus, my focus on the connection between public policy and distributional outcomes in this chapter provides a fairly straightforward extension of the macro politics model.

Examining the link between public policy and inequality is not only a direct extension of previous studies of U.S. macro politics, but can also be linked to power resources theory. The macro politics model and power resources theory overlap quite neatly with respect to party control of government, and they also overlap with respect to the analysis of public policy.

Most conceptions of power resources theory consider public policy as an output that varies depending on the constellation of power resources. Under this view the state is an instrument for the exercise of power resources, and indicators of power resources such as left party strength in government are used to explain state action. Probably owing in large part to a lack of comparable cross-national data, however, public policy is not directly observed or measured in previous studies. While such analyses would almost undoubtedly have occurred in the existing power resources literature if reliable cross-national data were available, these studies rely instead on observing the connection between power resource variables such as party control and policy consequence variables such as government redistribution. The power resources tradition essentially examines public policy indirectly by treating it as an unobserved variable that is used by those with power resources to accomplish their distributional objectives.

Given that I am working in the context of a single country in which cross-national data comparability is not an issue, I am able to examine public policy directly as an indicator of power resources, which intervenes between distributional outcomes and the more traditional indicators of political power resources. I view the policies enacted by government as an additional, more causally proximate link between power resources and distributional outcomes. As I alluded to in the previous chapter, parties are certainly not the only indicators of power resources. The poor have greater power resources if excellent individual candidates with strong left ideologies that support programs to benefit the poor run for office, strong advocates of welfare programs hold important leadership positions in the legislative branch, or interest groups representing lower class interests are particularly strong. Like left party control, these power resources should produce changes in policy. Thus, assessing policy as a power resource moves the conceptualization and measurement of power resources beyond just party control. In sum, analyzing the connection between public policy and distributional outcomes provides a direct extension of the macro politics model and a more comprehensive examination of power resources theory.[2]

---

[2] Some would argue that policy cannot be examined in a power resources framework because it is endogenous. While it is no doubt true that policy is endogenous in the

As in Chapter 4, I examine two broad mechanisms through which government policy can influence income inequality. The first is explicit redistribution, which occurs whenever government takes money from some and gives it to others. The results of the previous chapter, along with many other studies in the power resources literature, show that the direct effect of left party control of government is greater redistribution and, via this mechanism, less income inequality (Bradley et al. 2003, Hicks and Swank 1984, Sawyer 1976, Van Arnhem and Schotsman 1982). The connection analyzed in this chapter – between public policy and redistribution – has not been explicitly examined. Given the previous finding in the macro politics literature that Democratic control produces liberal policy enactments (Erikson et al. 2002), the clear expectation is that leftward shifts in public policy will produce more redistribution.

I also examine a mechanism for distributional policy consequences that, as discussed in the previous chapter, is related to power resources theory but has not been rigorously assessed – actions that modify market outcomes. Building on the idea that lower class power resources influence distributional outcomes through a governmental and market component, I posit that public policy influences distributional outcomes through a governmental and market component. The governmental component is explicit redistribution, and the market component is market conditioning. Power resources theory argues that distributional outcomes are central to state activity, and if this is the case then the state should use the tools of both explicit redistribution and market conditioning to influence the distribution of income. An ideological change in public policy should yield consistent distributional effects via explicit redistribution and market conditioning. That is, a shift to the left in policy should produce greater redistribution and reductions in government conditioned market inequality (see Figure 5.1).

---

sense that party control influences it, it is also appropriate to think of policy as an additional and more causally proximate indicator of political power resources. This is not unlike the examination of both union strength and left party control as indicators of power resources in the existing power resources literature. Comparative work shows that union strength produces left party control (it is endogenous), but a great deal of important work examining both of these power resource variables has been rightly embraced.

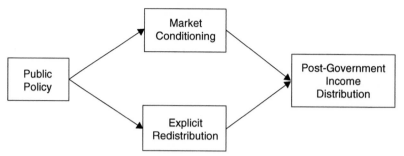

FIGURE 5.1. Policy and Two Mechanisms of Distributional Impact

CONCEPTUALIZING AND MEASURING MACRO POLICY: MICRO VS. MACRO

To this point, I have often mentioned the term public policy but have said little about how to define it. In this analysis, policy is conceptualized as the sum total of policies enacted by government. This conceptualization has three important characteristics. First, it is only interested in important and substantive change. Some activities by policymakers represent failed policy attempts or symbolic activities designed for an audience, but laws embody government policies that at least have the potential to influence peoples' lives. Second, policy is viewed cumulatively – not as newly developed each year, but the result of modifications to previous decisions. Changes occur at the margin while most previous policy decisions remain in effect. These marginal changes are what should influence the path of distributional outcomes. Finally, this conceptualization of policy is highly aggregated. While it is common to take a particularistic view of policy with each set of policies representing government's response to a particular set of issues, a focus on individual policies is not satisfying in the broader theoretical context of the macro politics model.

My focus on policy at the macro level is what distinguishes it most clearly from previous studies of public policy and distributional outcomes, so I want to say a bit more about this aspect of the macro policy concept. Traditionally, analysts interested in public policy divide policy into individual pieces or domains. Questions are framed in terms of "does policy X influence outcome Y?" In the context of distributional outcomes, typical issues are the effect of transfer spending on distributional outcomes or the impact of welfare reform on income inequality.

The concern with conceptualizing policy as an aggregate phenomenon in the context of distributional outcomes is that such a conceptualization might include policies unrelated to income inequality. One hypothetical response to this concern might be to conceptualize public policy at a more aggregate level than individual policies, but not move to the highest level of aggregation. For example, this line of thinking might lead to examining subsets of policy. One subset might focus on policies that have distributional goals. A second subset might focus on policies that do not. Arguably, conceptualizing such multiple subsets of policy could even be used to generate measures of redistributional policy and market conditioning policy that are closely connected to the mechanisms of distributional impact suggested by my application of the macro politics model and power resources theory to income inequality in the United States.

I have selected the more highly aggregated conception of public policy for two primary reasons. First, the theory of distributional outcomes that I have outlined argues that nearly every governmental policy either redistributes income or conditions markets. I am agnostic about which micro policies actually generate different distributional outcomes, but the theory suggests that nearly all micro policies have the *potential* to impact distributional outcomes via the market conditioning mechanism. One cannot fully ascertain the distributional impact of government through the combination of redistribution and market conditioning by examining just *subsets* of policy. Thus, the macro policy conception is more consistent with the theory of distributional outcomes that I have laid out and the macro politics model in general.

Second, examining the ideological tone of macro policy provides an indicator of lower class power resources that would not be evident with a more particularistic view of policy. Power resources theory often thinks of micro policies as tools that those with power resources can use to achieve desired outcomes. Left party control of government is an indicator of lower class power resources, and left parties tweak the tools of policy to change outcomes. Moving the conception of policy to the macro level allows us to think of policy not just as a set of individual tools that can change distributional outcomes, such as transfer payments and job training, but as an indicator of power resources in themselves. So, macro policy in one sense can be thought of as a variable that intervenes between party control of government and distributional outcomes. But the left-right content of macro policy could be thought of as more than a mere intervening variable – it might also be considered an additional and more precise indicator of lower class power resources.

Macro policy as an indicator of power resources may be particularly appropriate in the context of the United States. Despite the fact that a connection between party control and distributional outcomes was discovered in the analysis of the previous chapter, class-based interests are not well-consolidated. While the Democratic Party is clearly more oriented toward lower class interests than the Republican Party, class-based partisan differences are not as clear in the United States as they are in the European democracies where power resources theory has been developed and typically tested. The reality of American politics is that parties have been less disciplined (despite recent changes) and more factionalized (often along regional lines) than most of their European counterparts. In such a context, it seems unlikely that party control is the best indicator of political power resources, and it increases the utility of the macro policy concept.

With this aggregate conception of policy in mind, I use a measure of policy developed by Erikson et al. (2002). This measure examines important policy change by focusing on the crucial public laws identified by David Mayhew (2005). From this list, laws related to domestic policy with national impact are coded as to whether they were viewed as expanding (liberal) or contracting (conservative) government at the time they were passed. Laws that were ambiguous in their expansion versus contraction of government were coded as neutral and do not contribute to the policy change captured in this measure. Liberal legislation is counted +1, conservative legislation −1, and exceptionally important laws (as defined by Mayhew) are counted +2 or −2. Each year since 1947, a score is produced by summing liberal minus conservative legislation – this is annual policy change.

The current level of policy is produced by accumulating annual policy change over time. A net liberal shift in policy produces a positive change in this policy measure. Since the late 1940s, the most important policy changes have usually led to government expansion. In essence, then, the debate in the United States has not been literally about the contraction versus expansion of government, but about how much government should expand in response to the problems that develop in an increasingly complex society. In the context of the post-World War II United States, conservatives have not regularly offered proposals that would contract government. Rather, they have opposed new government expansion. Given this, a measure that focuses simply on the expansion versus contraction of government does not appropriately capture policy as a result of the ideological conflicts occurring in the governing system of the United States.

Since my interest is in determining which side of the ideological debate is winning in political conflict, it is more appropriate to examine the accumulation of policy relative to the long-term trend of government expansion. During the period under analysis (1947–2000), there was an average of 2.19 new laws passed each year that expanded government activity. The detrended measure of policy utilized in this analysis removes the trend of 2.19, rising only when the net increase in government-expanding laws exceeds 2.19 and declining when the net increase falls below 2.19. I will refer to this measure as policy liberalism. It is charted in Figure 5.2 from 1947 to 2000 and shows that the major turning points of policy occur in some expected places. A

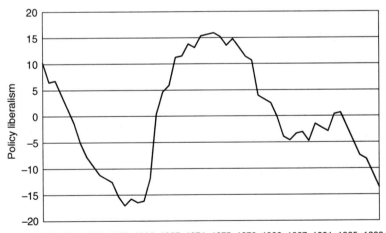

FIGURE 5.2. Policy Liberalism (Detrended), 1947–2000

sharp liberal turn in policy took place in the early 1960s as Lyndon Johnson began his Great Society program, while policy turned in a conservative direction around the time of Reagan's election to the presidency, and another sharp turn toward the right happened after the Republican takeover of Congress in 1994.

POLICY AND DISTRIBUTIONAL OUTCOMES, 1947–2000

The theoretical framework of this book suggests a particular set of relationships between policy liberalism and distributional outcomes. Liberal policy is expected to increase redistribution and decrease pre-redistribution inequality, thereby decreasing overall inequality by definition. With these expectations in mind, I conduct a time-series analysis of the connections between policy liberalism, pre-redistribution inequality, and redistribution. The basic contours of the analysis are similar to that conducted in the previous chapter. First, I extend existing analyses of the political determinants of overt government redistribution by examining the connection between policy liberalism and redistribution. Then, I examine the relationship about which previous research has said the least – policy liberalism and pre-redistribution inequality. This part of the analysis sheds light on whether market conditioning influences income inequality. Throughout the analysis, I again apply single equation error correction models (ECMs) to data from 1947 to 2000.

Policy Liberalism and Government Redistribution

I found in the previous chapter that there is a direct link between the party controlling the White House and the amount by which government programs reduce inequality. While a variety of control variables were included in initial models of government redistribution, in the end only unemployment and the elderly population were linked to government redistribution in addition to party control. Given knowledge based on previous research that party control of policymaking institutions is connected to the ideological tone of policymaking in Washington (Erikson et al. 2002) and the close conceptual linkage between party control and policymaking in the theoretical framework of my analysis, the final model of redistribution estimated in the previous chapter, with policy liberalism substituted for Democratic control of the presidency, provides a useful framework for the analysis of policy and redistribution.[3]

Table 5.1 presents this model, which reports an ECM of changes in redistribution regressed on lagged levels and current changes in unemployment and the aged population, in addition to lagged levels and changes in policy liberalism. This model answers two straightforward questions. First, does policy liberalism increase government redistribution? Second, is the timing of the policy effect similar to that of party control? The results support an affirmative answer to both questions.

TABLE 5.1. *Public Policy and Government Redistribution, 1947–2000*

Independent Variables	Δ Redistribution
Error Correction Rate	-0.38^{***} (0.12)
Political Power Resources	
$\quad\Delta$ Policy Liberalism$_{t-1}$	0.01 (0.07)
$\quad$Policy Liberalism$_{t-1}$	0.05^{**} (0.02)
Labor Market Factors	
$\quad\Delta$ % Unemployed$_t$	0.53^{**} (0.21)
$\quad$% Unemployed$_{t-1}$	0.57^{*} (0.29)
Demographic Factors	
$\quad\Delta$ % Aged 65+$_t$	-1.56 (4.57)
$\quad$% Aged 65+$_{t-1}$	2.93^{***} (0.94)
Response to Inequality	
$\quad\Delta$ Pre-Redist. Inequality$_t$	4.94^{***} (0.72)
Constant	-14.32 (5.25)
Adj. R^2	0.77
N	52

Two-tailed significance levels: $^{**}p \leq 0.05$; $^{***}p \leq 0.01$.

Note: Table entries are time series regression coefficients representing a single-equation error correction model with standard errors in parentheses.

[3] Estimating models with a wide variety of control variables included in the previous chapter does not substantively change the results for policy liberalism reported here. These more detailed results with all controls included are excluded because they are parallel to those in the previous chapter and add nothing of substance to the simpler results reported here.

As with party control, policy liberalism has a positive influence on government redistribution that is distributed over time. A one point positive shift in policy liberalism (an additional liberal law relative to the long-term trend) produces no immediate impact on redistribution. However, this liberal shift does create a disequilibrium in which redistribution is too low relative to policy liberalism. Beginning in the year after the initial liberal shift, redistribution begins to respond by increasing 0.05 points. In other words, a liberal shift in policy has the short-term effect of increasing the percentage by which government reduces inequality via explicit redistribution by 0.05 percentage points. Substantively, this is a small impact, and even the long-run multiplier effect of a unit increase in policy liberalism on redistribution is a mere 0.13 percentage point increase.[4] Still, this impact is consistent with the predictions of power resources theory and the macro politics model and, after all, is the impact of just one additional liberal law in a given year. Thus, the importance of the connection between policy and redistribution is real.

The results of the policy model are nearly identical to that of the party control model estimated previously. Policy, like party control, has an impact on redistribution that is distributed over time through the error correction component. As in the party control model, unemployment produces a positive and statistically significant increase in redistribution in both the short and long term. The same is true for the long-term impact of the aged population via the error correction component. A one point increase in the percentage of the population that is aged 65 and older increases redistribution by well over seven points ($2.93/0.38 = 7.71$). In this model, however, the aged population has no short-term impact on redistribution. This is likely due to the more nuanced measure of the ideological direction of government action and lower class power resources utilized here. Change in control of the presidency can typically only occur every four years, whereas policy liberalism can shift from year to year. This makes it less likely that variables such as the aged population will make a difference for redistribution in the short term. Still, the results here for party control and policy liberalism are largely comparable.

---

[4] A more in-depth discussion of the substantive size of policy impact on redistribution occurs in the next chapter.

Policy Liberalism and Pre-Redistribution Inequality

As with party control of government, the ideological tone of policy outputs directly affect government redistribution. Analyzing the connection between policy liberalism and pre-redistribution inequality provides information about whether the effects of party control and policy are also parallel with respect to the market conditioning mechanism.

In Table 5.2, I present this analysis. As in the analysis of redistribution, I begin with the final model of pre-redistribution inequality estimated in the previous chapter, substituting policy liberalism for party control of the presidency. In addition to policy liberalism as an indicator of political power resources and union strength as an indicator of market power resources, unemployment and immigration are included as control variables. It is worth noting, however, that including the wide variety of other controls that were considered in the analysis of the previous chapter does not change the substance of the reported results.

TABLE 5.2. *Public Policy and Pre-Redistribution Inequality, 1947–2000*

Independent Variables	Δ Pre-Redistribution Inequality
Error Correction Rate	-0.84^{***} (0.13)
Political Power Resources	
Δ Policy Liberalism$_{t-1}$	-0.03^{***} (0.01)
Market Power Resources	
Δ % Unionized$_{t-1}$	0.04 (0.06)
% Unionized$_{t-1}$	-0.10^{***} (0.02)
Labor Market Factors	
Δ % Unemployed$_{t-1}$	0.05 (0.03)
% Unemployed$_{t-1}$	0.10^{***} (0.02)
Demographic Factors	
Δ % New Immigrants$_{t-1}$	-0.84^{***} (0.21)
% New Immigrants$_{t-1}$	0.57^{***} (0.18)
Adj. R^2	0.54
N	52

Two-tailed significance levels: $^*p \leq 0.10$; $^{**}p \leq 0.05$; $^{***}p \leq 0.01$.

Note: Table entries are time series regression coefficients representing a single-equation error correction model with standard errors in parentheses.

The results reported in Table 5.2 are unequivocal. Policy liberalism and union strength, the variables of central theoretical interest, have significant effects on income inequality. Liberal shifts in public policy produce reductions in pre-redistribution inequality, as does union strength. Substantively, a one point increase in policy liberalism (i.e., the average number liberal laws passed each year is exceeded by one, representing a 1 percent change based on the variance of this series) reduces the ratio of the aggregate income of the top income quintile to the bottom two quintiles by 0.03 points. This amounts to approximately a 2.5 percent change. So, a 1 percent increase in policy liberalism produces a 3 percent reduction in inequality. This is a substantively important impact, and given the nonstationarity of pre-redistribution inequality in terms of its time series properties, this influence of policy leads to a permanent change in distributional outcomes. That is, once inequality increases or decreases in response to a change in policy, that increase or decrease continues into the future until some countervailing force emerges. Importantly, since the dependent variable in this analysis captures inequality that exists prior to the explicit effects of government redistribution, this shows that market conditioning is an avenue through which policy influences distributional outcomes. While government overtly uses transfer policies to change the income distribution, policy also influences inequality before explicit transfers. In addition, the distributional consequences of policy via market conditioning are felt quickly since the policy effect is fully captured in the short term.

CONCLUSION

Previous theoretical development of the macro politics model has focused on a variety of macro-social phenomena in the United States. Income inequality, however, has not been previously analyzed as a component of the U.S. macro polity. Instead, the policies produced by the U.S. national government are essentially analyzed as the final product of the political process. In this chapter I linked insights from power resources theory and the macro politics model to generate expectations about the connection between the ideological direction of policy outputs and distributional outcomes.

The central question of this chapter was whether policy liberalism reduces income inequality via redistribution and/or market conditioning. The answer is yes on both counts. When public policy shifts toward the left, the most immediate effect is a reduction in pre-redistribution inequality – the distribution of income produced primarily by decisions made in more or less open markets. Market decision makers observe a shift in policy and quickly change their behavior to adapt to the new reality of government policy. But this is not the only distributional consequence for a change in public policy. A shift to the left in policy also creates a disequilibrium in which redistribution is too low when compared to the ideological tone of policy. At the rate of about 38 percent each year after the policy shock, redistribution increases to catch up with policy, eventually increasing government redistribution by 0.13 percentage points for every new liberal law (relative to the trend) enacted. Interestingly, the effect of policy liberalism on pre-redistribution inequality occurs more quickly than its effect on explicit redistribution. This means that the explicit redistributive impact of government is slower to respond to macro political change than is the more nebulous impact that the state achieves through market conditioning.

While the analysis in this chapter answered many questions, there are still a few matters that remain unresolved. Is it possible that pre-redistribution inequality responds to redistribution, thus generating a form of reciprocal causation that has not been accounted for in the analysis to this point? Are there indirect effects of politics on inequality that manifest themselves via the labor market? What is the overall substantive impact of politics on the distribution of income in the United States? I turn to these issues in the next chapter.

6

Putting the Pieces Together: Who Gets
What and How

The previous two chapters tested the central predictions of power resources theory and the macro politics model for distributional outcomes in the United States. Chapter 4 demonstrated that Democratic control of the presidency is associated with lower levels of income inequality, and this is the case because explicit redistribution is greater and market inequality is lower when a Democrat is in the White House as opposed to a Republican. This is consistent with the main predictions of power resources theory and my extension of it to the U.S. case. Chapter 5 focused on public policy as a central variable in the macro politics model and assessed whether leftward shifts in macro policy produce reductions in inequality. The evidence supported the conclusion that the macro politics model can be extended to distributional outcomes. Like Democratic Party control, public policy liberalism reduces inequality via both market conditioning and explicit redistribution.

The models examined in the previous two chapters are depicted in the form of a path model in Figure 6.1. The light solid lines are the paths analyzed in both Chapters 4 and 5. The heavy dotted lines represent paths examined in Chapter 4 alone, and the heavy solid lines are the paths examined in Chapter 5 alone. The essential item to note from this diagram is that the analysis to this point has treated all explanatory factors as influencing distributional outcomes in a single causal stage. These models are interesting and provide clear evidence in support of a combination of power resources theory and the macro politics model. But when added together they are more than the sum of their parts.

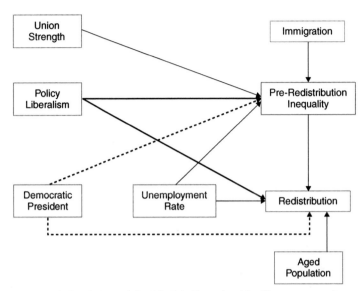

FIGURE 6.1. A Depiction of the Models Examined in Chapters 4 and 5

In this chapter, I combine these previous models in order to answer questions about the distributional process that have been unexplored in the analysis to this point.

A MORE COMPLETE PICTURE OF POLITICS AND INCOME INEQUALITY

The strategy of modeling all explanatory variables in a single causal stage is an appropriate way to determine the direct effects of political factors on distributional outcomes, but this likely fails to capture fully and accurately the overall impact of politics on the distributional process. Specifically, this approach leaves three important unanswered questions. First, while it is clear that macro political dynamics have clear and direct effects on distributional outcomes, examining the effect of politics in a single stage leaves open the question of whether political variables have indirect effects via their influence on other explanatory factors. An indirect effect might occur, for example, if Democrats reduce unemployment, which in turn reduces pre-redistribution inequality. The second remaining question is related to the linkages between pre-redistribution inequality and redistribution

– how does pre-redistribution inequality respond to explicit redistribution? While pre-redistribution inequality was included as a control variable in models of redistribution, the potential effect of redistribution on pre-redistribution inequality has not been examined. Third, the analysis has focused only on explanatory factors hypothesized to have a direct impact on income inequality. In the context of the macro politics model, it is important to learn whether or not distributional outcomes are responsive to changes in mass preferences. If a change in public opinion can be linked to distributional outcomes, this effect will be indirect, coming via representational mechanisms that influence the composition of government and public policy.

Indirect Effects of Politics via Employment Policies

The models in Chapters 4 and 5 examine the direct impact of the theoretically central variables while controlling for potentially confounding factors. For example, in Chapter 4, the effects of union strength and party control of government (power resources variables) on pre-redistribution inequality were estimated while controlling for labor market and demographic factors. This type of analysis is useful for determining whether power resources and macro politics variables are *directly* linked to distributional outcomes while controlling for other potential explanations. The results to this point demonstrate that such a direct link does, in fact, exist between politics and distributional outcomes. Along with the controls for unemployment, pre-redistribution inequality, and the aged population, party control of government and policy liberalism have an impact on redistribution. Similarly, the central theoretical variables of party control, policy liberalism, and union strength are directly connected to pre-redistribution inequality while controlling for economic and demographic factors.

Thus far, the analysis leads to the conclusion that party control and public policy have an influence on inequality via both market conditioning and redistribution, but there is no basis on which to make a judgment regarding the overall impact of politics on distributional outcomes. The approach of the previous two chapters estimates only the direct impact of politics on redistribution and pre-redistribution inequality, but not necessarily the total impact. The total impact could be identical to the direct impact, but this would require an important assumption – namely, that the political variables having a direct impact on distributional outcomes do not also influence other explanatory variables. This assumption is almost certainly incorrect with respect to unemployment. Numerous previous studies have found that party control of government influences unemployment rates (Alesina and Rosenthal 1995, Erikson et al. 2002, Hibbs 1987, Hibbs and Dennis 1988). The analysis to this point, however, does not explore what impact political factors have on income inequality via this indirect causal path.

Thus, the first complication that I introduce in this chapter is the consideration of indirect political effects via unemployment. Rather than treating unemployment like other control variables, it will be treated as an endogenous variable that not only explains distributional outcomes, but also is explained by politics. This will provide a basis to estimate any additional impact that political variables have via their influence on unemployment. Based on previous research, the expectation is that Democratic control of government and policy liberalism decrease unemployment. Given that reductions in unemployment decrease pre-redistribution inequality, the indirect impact of political factors should augment their direct equalizing impact via market conditioning. The indirect impact of political factors on redistribution, however, should moderate their direct impact, since any reduced unemployment generated by Democratic control or policy liberalism would reduce redistribution. This would counteract the increase in redistribution that is produced by the direct effect of these variables.

Linkages Between Redistribution and Pre-Redistribution Inequality

A second issue that has not been fully addressed in Chapters 4 and 5 is the connection between pre-redistribution inequality and redistribution. In my models of redistribution, I included pre-redistribution inequality as a control variable based on the idea that higher levels of existing inequality will induce more redistributive effort to narrow the gap between the top and the bottom of the income distribution. This is in line with recent studies of redistribution (Bradley et al. 2003) as well as the classic political economy model of Meltzer and Richard (1981).

These earlier results showed that the impact of pre-redistribution inequality on redistribution is strong and positive. This in and of itself indicates the existence of an indirect path (in addition to that via unemployment discussed above) between political factors and redistribution. That is, we know that power resources and macro politics variables are directly connected to pre-redistribution inequality. Democratic control of the presidency and leftward shifts in policy reduce pre-redistribution inequality. Furthermore, the models in the two previous chapters show that this reduction in pre-redistribution inequality, in turn, reduces redistribution. Thus, there is an indirect path between political factors and redistribution. This indirect path should be considered alongside the indirect effects that occur via unemployment.

While the impact of pre-redistribution inequality on redistribution was considered in the earlier analysis, the potential reverse connection was not explored. That is, I have not yet considered the possibility that redistribution increases pre-redistribution inequality. The main reason that this possibility has not been considered to this point is that the comparative evidence argues against such a connection. Most recently, Bradley et al. (2003) provided direct evidence on this point when they found no connection between welfare state generosity and pretax and transfer inequality. Despite the existing comparative evidence, however, it is important to consider the possibility that redistribution influences pre-redistribution inequality in the context of the liberal U.S. welfare state. Furthermore, unintended effects of redistribution on pre-redistribution inequality may eliminate any gains in equality produced by left parties and policies if more redistribution results in increases in market inequality.

Critics of the welfare state and some public economists have made this argument explicit. Browning (2002) discusses seven general arguments against redistribution, and three of these arguments are related to the idea that those at the bottom of the income distribution are made worse off by redistribution. One of the main mechanisms by which redistribution might increase pre-redistribution inequality is via work effort. Basic microeconomic theory predicts that providing someone with a transfer payment will produce a reduction in their private labor market effort. Thus, the benefits to a poor individual of a redistributive government benefit will be at least partially offset by reduced work effort. Several economic studies have found evidence consistent with this reduced work effort hypothesis in the United States (Danziger et al. 1981, Moffitt 1992). However, these studies do not directly examine the impact of redistribution on market income inequality.

Thus, accounting for the possibility of a two-way relationship between redistribution and pre-redistribution inequality will provide not only a more accurate assessment of power resources theory and the macro politics model, but will also provide new evidence related to economic theories of distributional outcomes.

Macro Politics and the Public Mood

The third and final question left unanswered by the approach utilized in the previous two chapters relates to the role of public opinion in the macro politics model. The previous models were concerned only with estimating the impact of variables that have a direct effect on the dependent variable. A group of independent variables are inserted on the right-hand side of a regression equation, and those with significant coefficients are interpreted as influencing the dependent variable while statistically controlling for all the other independent variables. At times, however, there are variables of theoretical interest that have no *direct* effect on the outcome variable that may have only an *indirect* influence via their effect on other factors that do have a direct impact.

This is precisely the situation that may be present with regard to the macro politics model and distributional outcomes. As discussed earlier, previous work in the macro politics tradition has been primarily concerned with public policy as the outcome of the governing system. One of the goals of my work, of course, is to extend the macro politics model to distributional outcomes by examining the connection between policy and income inequality. The analysis in Chapter 5 accomplished just that. However, one of the most interesting and important implications of extending the macro politics model to distributional outcomes has not been assessed – does the public mood influence societal outcomes?

When earlier macro politics research is combined with my analysis, it appears likely that changes in public opinion produce an indirect impact on distributional outcomes. If shifts to the left in the public mood produce Democratic control of government and left policymaking, and these political variables in turn produce greater pre-redistribution equality and more government redistribution, then (at least indirectly) shifts to the left (or right) in public opinion produce lower (or higher) levels of income inequality. If true, this would be a fascinating finding with important implications for recent examinations of inequality and American democracy (Bartels 2006,

2008, Weissburg 2006). The third extension to the analysis that I will implement in this chapter, then, is an explicit consideration of public opinion as an indirect influence on distributional outcomes.

THE COMPREHENSIVE MODEL: A SIMULTANEOUS EQUATION APPROACH

The unexplored questions discussed to this point motivate three extensions to the previous analysis. First, the indirect effects of party control and public policy will be assessed by providing a more careful specification of the causal ordering of the explanatory variables. More specifically, I consider unemployment as a variable which not only affects distributional outcomes directly, but is also an intervening variable that creates additional causal paths for the impact of political power resources on redistribution and market inequality. In addition, I treat party control of government as causally prior to public policy rather than entering the model at the same stage. This is consistent with macro politics findings showing that party control is a determinant of public policy (Erikson et al. 2002). Second, the possibility of a two-way connection between redistribution and pre-redistribution inequality is examined. This provides a more appropriate estimate of the connection between these two variables, and also opens the possibility for further indirect causal paths between union strength, party control, public policy, and distributional outcomes. Third, I include a measure of aggregate public opinion as a determinant of party control and public policy to test the ability of changes in mass preferences to influence important economic outcomes.

Figure 6.2 depicts this final model that I examine in this chapter. This figure is arranged in a similar fashion to the earlier Figure 6.1, with the exception that public mood is added here. The heavier lines indicate connections that were not included in the earlier analysis, and the subscripts indicate the temporal arrangement of the variables. It is also useful to note that Figure 6.2 is a spatially rearranged depiction of the theoretical model originally outlined at the beginning of the book in Figure 1.8, with important economic and demographic control variables added here.

Two of the three wrinkles that I add to the analysis in this chapter are essentially about specification of causal ordering – namely considering

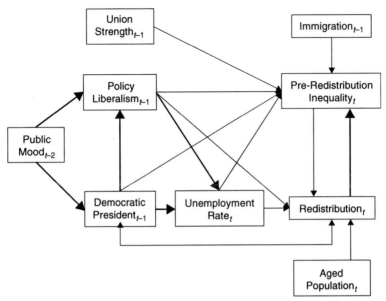

FIGURE 6.2. A Path Model of Macro Politics, Power Resources, and Distributional Outcomes (heavy lines indicate paths added to the analysis in this chapter)

both the direct *and* indirect effects of party control and policy and adding public mood to the model in order to assess its indirect effect on distributional outcomes. Using the impact of party control on pre-redistribution inequality as an example helps to illustrate the idea of direct and indirect effects. Each arrow in Figure 6.2 represents the impact of one variable on another. There is an arrow, for example, that runs from "Democratic President" to "Pre-Redistribution Inequality." This is a direct effect, because the path of the arrow is not interrupted by other variables. There is also an indirect path (this path is only hypothesized at this point) between party control and pre-redistribution inequality that runs through unemployment, which would be called an intervening variable. This is the case because an arrow runs not only between "Democratic President" and "Unemployment," but also from "Unemployment" to "Pre-Redistribution Inequality." Indirect effects occur whenever there is a path linking one variable to another and this path is interrupted by other intervening variables. One can see several potential indirect effects hypothesized in Figure 6.2.

Through statistical analysis, it is possible to calculate the magnitude of these direct and indirect effects, which can then be combined to calculate total effects. The introduction of direct and indirect effects to the model does not fundamentally alter the econometric techniques applied. Accounting for the direct and indirect effects of a variable simply requires additional error correction models (ECMs) estimated in the usual way. Continuing with the example of the impact of party control on pre-redistribution inequality, the direct effect of policy could be estimated in just one ECM like this:

$$\Delta \text{Pre}_t = \alpha_0 + \alpha_1 \text{Pre}_{t-1} + \beta_0 \Delta \text{DemPres}_{t-1} + \beta_1 \text{DemPres}_{t-1}$$
$$+ \beta_2 \Delta \text{Unemp}_t + \beta_3 \text{Unemp}_{t-1} + \epsilon_t \qquad (6.1)$$

This, in fact, is a simplified version of a model taken directly from Chapter 4, with the difference being that union strength and immigration are dropped here for the sake of simplicity. The direct effect of Democratic control of the presidency on pre-redistribution inequality could be computed by the short-term (β_0) or long-term (β_1/α_1) impact of party control. But if we wish to examine the potential indirect effect of party control via unemployment, a further model must be estimated:

$$\Delta \text{Unemp}_t = \gamma_0 + \gamma_1 \text{Unemp}_{t-1} + \lambda_0 \Delta \text{DemPres}_{t-1}$$
$$+ \lambda_1 \text{DemPres}_{t-1} + \rho_t \qquad (6.2)$$

If party control is found to have a significant influence on unemployment, then the indirect effect of party control on inequality via unemployment could be calculated by multiplying the effect of party control on unemployment by the effect of unemployment on pre-redistribution inequality.[1] The total effect, then, could be determined by summing the direct and indirect effects.

Much of the model depicted in Figure 6.2 could be estimated via a series of error correction models for each of the endogenous variables: pre-redistribution inequality, redistribution, unemployment,

---

[1] Path coefficients are traditionally presented as standardized effects when calculating direct and indirect effects. It is a simple matter to switch between standardized and unstandardized effects. Standardized coefficients can be computed from unstandardized coefficients as follows: $\beta_s = \beta_u * \sigma_x/\sigma_y$, where σ_x and σ_y refer to the standard deviation of the explanatory and outcome variables, respectively.

and policy liberalism. However, the more complex model assessed in this chapter does require a few modifications to these econometric methods because of the two-way causation hypothesized between redistribution and pre-redistribution inequality. More technically, since reciprocal causation is hypothesized between redistribution and pre-redistribution inequality, any regression of redistribution on pre-redistribution inequality and vice-versa could produce biased parameter estimates due to correlation between the error term and an explanatory variable. To overcome this problem, I estimate a system of error correction equations based on the above path diagram utilizing three-stage least squares. Using three-stage least squares resolves the bias introduced by reciprocal causation between redistribution and pre-redistribution inequality and provides for appropriate estimates of the direct and indirect effects of power resources and macro politics variables. However, application of this estimation procedure in no way limits my ability to account for the time dynamics present in the data. I am simply re-estimating the models of the previous two chapters using procedures that account for both time dynamics and potential reciprocal causation.

Using the results of the earlier chapters as a guide to determine which explanatory variables to include for each dependent variable, the system of equations that I estimate via three-stage least squares is as follows:[2]

$$\Delta Y_1 = \alpha_0 + \alpha_1 Y_1 + \beta_0 \Delta Y_2 + \beta_1 \Delta Y_3 + \beta_2 Y_3 + \beta_3 \Delta X_3 + \beta_4 X_3$$
$$+ \beta_5 \Delta X_2 + \beta_6 X_2 + \beta_7 \Delta X_5 + \beta_8 \Delta X_6 + \epsilon_1 \qquad (6.3)$$

---

[2] Policy liberalism was initially included as an explanation of unemployment, but was found to be insignificant and was dropped from the analysis. The equations below do not include a path from policy to unemployment in order to avoid additional complexity. As in any simultaneous equation model, it is important to discuss the identification of the model. Identification refers to the question of whether there is enough information in the data analyzed to estimate the unknown quantities in the model. If a model is not identified then it cannot be estimated properly. Oftentimes it is straightforward to see that a set of simultaneous equations is identified, but in models with such a large number of coefficients and reciprocal paths, identification is not so obvious. In an identified model, each equation has at least as many exogenous variables (those that do not appear on the left-hand side of any equation) excluded on the right-hand side as it has endogenous variables (those that appear on the left-hand side of any equation in the system) included on the right-hand side. Only the

$$\Delta Y_2 = \alpha_2 + \alpha_3 Y_2 + \beta_9 \Delta Y_1 + \beta_{10} \Delta X_4 + \beta_{11} X_4 + \beta_{12} \Delta Y_3 + \beta_{13} Y_3$$
$$+ \beta_{14} \Delta X_5 + \beta_{15} X_5 + \beta_{16} \Delta X_6 + \beta_{17} X_6 + \epsilon_2 \tag{6.4}$$
$$\Delta Y_3 = \alpha_4 + \alpha_5 Y_3 + \beta_{18} \Delta X_5 + \beta_{19} X_5 + \epsilon_3 \tag{6.5}$$

In addition, to examine the paths between public mood, party control, and policy, I estimate the following equations separately using standard time series techniques since these dependent variables are fully exogenous to the system above and need not be included in the three-stage least squares estimation:[3]

$$\Delta X_5 = \alpha_6 + \alpha_7 X_5 + \beta_{20} \Delta X_1 + \beta_{21} X_1 + \epsilon_4 \tag{6.6}$$
$$\Delta X_6 = \alpha_8 + \alpha_9 X_6 + \beta_{22} \Delta X_5 + \beta_{23} X_1 + \epsilon_5 \tag{6.7}$$

where, for all equations:

Y_1 = Pre-Redistribution Inequality$_t$

Y_2 = Redistribution$_t$

Y_3 = Unemployment$_t$

X_1 = Public Mood Liberalism$_{t-2}$

X_2 = Union Strength$_{t-1}$

first two equations in the system estimated here include endogenous variables on the right-hand side. In the first equation, two endogenous variables (ΔY_2 and ΔY_3) are included on the right-hand side (lagged levels are considered pre-determined since they only appear on the right-hand side) and four exogenous variables are excluded (ΔX_4, X_4, X_5, and X_6). This equation is identified. The second equation also includes two endogenous variables on the right-hand side (ΔY_1 and ΔY_3) and excludes four exogenous variables (ΔX_3, X_3, ΔX_4, and Y_4), thus also being identified and rendering the system as a whole identified as well.

[3] These specifications largely mimic those examined by Erikson et al. (2002), with the exception that their analysis examined election outcomes as the Democratic vote share while I examine the outcome as a dichotomy. Though these equations are both estimated using standard time series OLS, the results can be reproduced in substance by utilizing either logit or probit to estimate the results for party control. I present the OLS results for ease of presentation, given that discussing logit or probit results in the context of a path analysis would greatly limit substantive interpretation. Regardless, only the discussion of the impact of the public mood could be influenced by this simplification. Given the largely parallel substantive results using logit and probit, any impact on this discussion is a matter of degree rather than kind.

X_3 = Immigration$_{t-1}$

X_4 = Aged Population$_t$

X_5 = Democratic President$_{t-1}$

X_6 = Policy Liberalism$_{t-1}$

This is a complicated set of equations, but they are essentially a mathematical representation of the diagram presented in Figure 6.2. Each of the equations above has a dependent variable on the left side of the equation and a series of explanatory variables on the right side. The dependent variables are simply those from Figure 6.2 that have arrows pointing toward them, and the independent variables are those from the figure that have arrows running away from them. The model itself is simply a combination of the models in Chapters 4 and 5 with a couple of straightforward additions (public mood and a path between party control and policy liberalism) that spring directly from previous studies in the macro politics tradition.

Results

While I will not go into great detail here about the specifics of three-stage least squares estimates since the primary purpose of this analysis is simply to provide the basis for calculating the total impact of political dynamics on distributional outcomes (which will be discussed below), it is encouraging to note that the first two columns of Table 6.1 in large part mirror the models of redistribution and pre-redistribution inequality analyzed in the previous two chapters. The coefficient estimates in the second column for redistribution, in fact, are nearly identical to those from Chapters 4 and 5. The direct effect of both Democratic control and left public policy is an increase in redistribution via the error correction mechanism. In fact, the only difference between this model and the one discussed in the previous chapters is that these coefficient estimates are actually slightly larger, though substantively similar. The model of pre-redistribution inequality reported in Column 1 also tells a story similar to that of Chapters 4 and 5. Lower class power resources and leftward shifts in macro political factors produce a direct effect of lower levels of pre-redistribution inequality. However, the coefficient estimates of the three-stage least squares model reported here are

TABLE 6.1. *Estimating a Structural Model of Distributional Outcomes*

Independent Variables	(1)	(2)	(3)	(4)	(5)
Error Correction Rate	−0.37***	−0.41***	−0.26***	n.a.	−0.25**
	(0.10)	(0.12)	(0.14)		(0.10)
Δ Democratic President$_{t-1}$	−0.17***	−0.36	−0.97**	2.07*	−0.30***
	(0.06)	(0.67)	(0.41)	(1.13)	(0.09)
Democratic President$_{t-1}$		1.22***	−0.54*		
		0.40	(0.29)		
Δ Policy Liberalism$_{t-1}$	−0.01**	0.06			
	(−0.006)	(0.06)			
Policy Liberalism$_{t-1}$		0.04*			
		(0.02)			
Δ % Unionized$_{t-1}$	0.02				
	(0.03)				
% Unionized$_{t-1}$	−0.05***				
	(0.01)				
Δ % Unemployed$_t$	0.00	0.77***			
	(0.02)	(0.21)			
% Unemployed$_{t-1}$	0.07***	0.78**			
	(0.02)	(0.31)			
Δ % Aged 65+$_t$		1.77			
		(3.79)			
% Aged 65+$_{t-1}$		3.21***			
		(0.98)			
Δ % Immigrants$_{t-1}$	−0.49***				
	(0.11)				
% Immigrants$_{t-1}$	0.29***				
	(0.09)				
Δ Public Mood$_t$					0.01
					(0.02)
Public Mood$_{t-1}$				0.20**	0.02*
				(0.09)	(0.01)
Δ Pre-Redist$_t$		4.65***			
		(0.90)			
Δ Redist$_t$	0.08**				
	(0.01)				
Constant	2.09***	−17.70***	1.71***	−12.15**	−1.16*
	(0.70)	(5.85)	(0.60)	(5.18)	(0.66)
R^2	0.86	0.82	0.33	0.20	0.20
N	52	52	52	48	48

Two-tailed significance levels: *$p \leq 0.10$; **$p \leq 0.05$; ***$p \leq 0.01$.

Note: Dependent variables by column are as follows: (1) Δ Pre-Redistribution Inequality, (2) Δ Redistribution, (3) Δ Unemployment, (4) Δ Policy Liberalism, and (5) Δ Democratic President. The first three columns report three-stage least squares coefficients representing single-equation error correction models with standard errors in parentheses. The final two columns report time series regression coefficients with standard errors in parentheses. Public mood (liberalism) is first available in 1952, limiting the number of years to 48 for models including public mood.

slightly smaller than those in the previous analysis. This makes sense given that an additional control for the amount of redistribution is added to the model here.

The third column of the table presents the results for unemployment, which were also estimated as part of the three-stage least squares system of equations. Consistent with previous studies, Democratic control of the White House decreases unemployment. Public policy, however, has no direct effect on unemployment independent of party control and is therefore dropped from the model. The last two columns of the table assess the effect of Stimson's (1999) public mood liberalism measure on party control of the presidency and policy liberalism. Liberal shifts in public opinion increase the likelihood of a Democratic presidency and increase the liberalism of public policy. These results indicate that public opinion has an indirect impact on distributional outcomes. The results also show that macro political factors have indirect paths of influence on distributional outcomes as well as a direct influence.

Perhaps the most interesting result in Table 6.1 is that we observe a reciprocal relationship between redistribution and pre-redistribution inequality. As we saw in the previous chapters, higher pre-redistribution inequality produces an increase in redistribution. This is evidenced by the model in Column 2, in which a one-unit change in pre-redistribution inequality produces an increase of 4.65 in redistribution. So, if the ratio of the income of the top income quintile to the bottom two income quintiles increases by one, the percentage reduction in inequality attributable to the first-order effects of explicit redistribution increases by more than 4.5 percentage points. This effect is likely due to the fact that when inequality goes up, eligibility for redistributive programs goes up at the same time. It would be inappropriate, however, to conclude that the link between pre-redistribution inequality and redistribution is merely due to economic downturns, for this connection remains even while controlling for business cycle indicators such as unemployment (and GDP and a variety of other indicators not shown in the analysis here). We must keep in mind that relative economic conditions indicated by income inequality are distinguishable from absolute economic outcomes like median income, unemployment, and GDP. For example, if the gap between the rich and poor is increasing dramatically it is possible for general economic indicators to be improving while, at the same time, there are more poor people eligible for means-tested programs. A second mechanism that might be at work here is public opinion. Voters may respond to increased inequality by demanding more redistribution, shifting their mood to the left, electing more Democrats, and pressuring even Republicans to provide more generous benefits. This is precisely the argument put forward by Meltzer and Richard (1981).

What is new here is that, consistent with microeconomic theory, the reverse is also true – redistribution conditions market outcomes, with greater redistributive impact by government pushing pre-redistribution inequality higher. More specifically, we see in Column 1 of the table that when redistribution increases by a full percentage point, pre-redistribution inequality is increased by 0.08 points. Remembering that the average change in pre-redistribution inequality is 0.22 points, this is a notable impact confirming that increasing redistribution can have unintended and undesirable side-effects.

These results have an important implication for what happens when a leftward shift occurs in the macro polity – that is, when a Democrat takes over the White House or policy liberalism increases. We know that such leftward shifts have the direct impact of reducing pre-redistribution inequality and increasing redistribution. Interestingly, though, these reductions in pre-redistribution inequality are partly offset by simultaneous increases in pre-redistribution inequality that are spawned indirectly by the increased redistribution. By the same token, these direct increases in redistribution can be reduced by the simultaneous reductions in redistribution generated indirectly by decreases in pre-redistribution inequality. Given these possibilities and the results from the models of unemployment, party control, and public policy, it is important to fully consider the direct and indirect impact of politics on redistribution and pre-redistribution inequality, as well as the overall impact of these variables on post government inequality.

In order to facilitate the calculation of the direct and indirect impact of macro politics, lower class power resources, labor market, and demographic factors, I present a path diagram of the full structural model in Figure 6.3. On each path I display the standardized combined short and long-term impact of the explanatory variable on the dependent variable, based on the coefficient estimates from

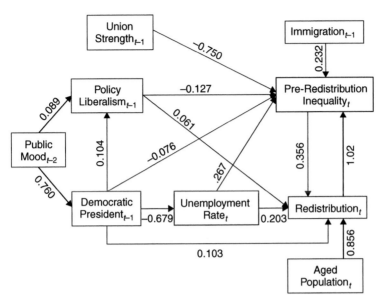

FIGURE 6.3. Path Diagram for Full Model, Standardized Short- and Long-Term Impact

Table 6.1. Insignificant coefficients are excluded from the diagram. For some paths, such as that between party control and pre-redistribution inequality, only a short-term impact is present. For others, like the path between union strength and pre-redistribution inequality, only an effect via the error correction component is present. In still other cases, like the impact of unemployment on redistribution, both short- and long-term effects are present. In all cases in which long-term effects are present, the long-term effect is the standardized effect that would be realized after the error correction is complete.

Comparing the Magnitude of Direct Effects

In the next section, I use these path coefficients to calculate the total effects of the explanatory variables on distributional outcomes. At this point, however, I want to focus on comparing the magnitude of the direct effects presented in the figure. Comparing the variables that directly influence redistribution, we find that the aged population is by far the strongest predictor, with an effect that is more than twice as large as the second most important explanatory factor, pre-redistribution inequality. Of the variables that are of central theoretical interest, both party control and policy have important direct effects on redistribution. However, their direct effects are small in comparison to factors such as unemployment and the aged population. Much of the effect of these political variables on redistribution occurs via indirect paths, and the indirect paths in most cases work against the direct effects. For example, the direct impact of a Democratic president on redistribution is positive. However, the indirect effect via unemployment is negative since Democratic presidents decrease unemployment which, in turn, decreases redistribution.

Switching focus to pre-redistribution inequality, we again see that party control and policy have direct effects that are much smaller than unemployment. As well, compared to the direct effect of immigration on pre-distribution inequality, the effect of party control is just one-third as large and the impact of policy liberalism is approximately half as large. In addition, many of the indirect effects of party control and public policy actually augment their direct effect. For example, the direct effect of Democratic control is -0.076, which is augmented by its indirect effect via unemployment. While redistribution has the single largest direct impact on pre-redistribution inequality, market power resources as indicated by union strength have the second largest impact. All in all, lower class power resources and macro politics are important predictors of both pre-redistribution inequality and redistribution, but the results are actually somewhat stronger for pre-redistribution inequality than redistribution. This again supports the conclusion that politics influences distributional outcomes more via the market conditioning mechanism than via redistribution in the United States.

Comparing the Magnitude of Total Effects

Even more useful than comparisons of the direct effects of the explanatory variables is a calculation of the total effects produced by the combined direct and indirect impact of each variable. These total effects are calculated for each explanatory variable in Table 6.2. The first column of the table reports the standardized and unstandardized total effect of each variable on pre-redistribution inequality, while the second column reports the same information for redistribution.

TABLE 6.2. *Total Effects (Standardized) of Power Resources, Macro Politics, Demographics, and Labor Market on Distributional Outcomes*

Independent Variables	Pre-Redistribution Inequality	Redistribution
Policy Liberalism	−0.011	0.036
	(−0.102)	(0.025)
Democratic President	−1.07	−5.76
	(−0.491)	(−0.202)
Union Strength	−0.193	−0.898
	(−1.18)	(−0.419)
Unemployment	0.549	4.43
	(0.773)	(0.478)
Immigration	1.23	5.73
	(0.364)	(0.130)
Aged Population	0.950	12.16
	(1.37)	(1.34)
Pre-Redistribution Inequality		7.30
		(0.559)
Redistribution	0.123	
	(1.601)	
Public Mood	−0.089	−0.611
	(−0.382)	(−0.200)

Note: Table entries are combined total short- and long-term effect of a one unit increase in the independent variable on the dependent variable. Standardized total effects are in parentheses. Effects are computed based on the path coefficients in Figure 6.3.

Substantively, the unstandardized total effect indicates how much the outcome variable will change after a one unit increase in the explanatory variable, while the standardized effect indicates the number of standard deviations by which the outcome will change for a one standard deviation change in the independent variable. All of these effects can be readily computed based on the path coefficients from Figure 6.3. The standardized impact of policy on pre-redistribution inequality, for example, can be calculated by adding its direct impact (−0.127) to its impact via redistribution (0.061 ∗ 1.02), for a total of −0.065. We must also account for the feedback effects produced by the causal loop between pre-redistribution inequality and redistribution. In other words, the direct impact of policy is augmented by the indirect effect that pre-redistribution inequality has on itself via redistribution, and the same can be said for the indirect effect of policy via redistribution. The causal loop provides a 57 percent augmentation to the usual effect, producing a total impact of $-0.065 * 1.57$, or -0.102. Converting this standardized effect to the original metrics of the variables provides the unstandardized impact of -0.011.

Examining the total impact of the explanatory variables in Table 6.2 leads to a variety of interesting conclusions. First, the effects of the central theoretical variables are as expected with regard to pre-redistribution inequality. Policy liberalism, Democratic control of the presidency, and union strength all work together to equalize market income. Substantively, the impact of party control is particularly striking. Switching from Republican to Democratic control produces more than a one-point reduction in pre-redistribution inequality. That is, the income ratio of the top quintile to the bottom two quintiles changes by over a point with a switch in party control. To give some idea of exactly how large this impact is, pre-redistribution inequality moves up or down by an average of just 0.22 each year. The impact of a switch in party control is nearly five times this amount of typical change. Using the standardized effects presented in parentheses in the table allows a comparison of the size of the impact of each variable and shows that the effect of party control (-0.491) is somewhat smaller in magnitude than unemployment (0.773) but is larger than the effect of immigration (0.364).

In addition, the combined impact of political power resources on market inequality is substantial, but not as strong as the impact of market power resources. The standardized impact of union strength, an indicator of market power resources, is -1.18 while the combined standardized impact of party control and policy, the indicators of political power resources, totals -0.593 $(-0.491 - 0.102)$. We also see that neither political power resources nor market power resources, considered separately, are as important as the logic of industrialism variable of the aged population. When market and power resources variables are combined, however, power resources have a substantially larger impact on pre-redistribution inequality than the impact of the aged population. Clearly, power resources variables are important predictors of distributional outcomes in their own right, side by side with other theoretical explanations.

The results are more surprising for redistribution. Previous research has focused almost entirely on the impact of politics on government redistribution, viewing redistribution as the primary path through which political contestation can influence distributional outcomes. The results of this final model do not support such a conclusion, which is a product of the fact that the analysis here examines income inequality as a two-stage process and explicitly considers the possibility of direct and indirect effects of macro political variables. In fact, when the direct and indirect effects of party control of the presidency on redistribution are considered, the effect is in the opposite direction of the prediction. Democratic control of the presidency actually *reduces* redistribution rather than increasing it. This result is counterintuitive on its face, runs against conventional wisdom, and tells a different story than previous studies of redistribution.

The best way to understand this result is to focus on the fact that government can use multiple mechanisms to influence distributional outcomes, and these mechanisms feed back on one another. When government conditions the market in a way that increases inequality, this market conditioning feeds back onto the redistributive state. This feedback actually increases the need for redistribution and nudges the redistributive impact of government higher. If eligibility requirements for explicitly redistributive programs remain steady over time while those at the bottom become worse-off due to increased government conditioned market inequality, government will redistribute more as this change occurs. Turning to the numbers, we see this play out by again examining Figure 6.3. Democratic control of the presidency directly increases redistribution, with a standardized coefficient of 0.103. But now look at its effect via unemployment. Democrats decrease unemployment, and decreased unemployment leads to decreased redistribution. Democrats also reduce pre-redistribution inequality, and a reduction in pre-redistribution inequality translates into a reduction of redistribution. When direct and indirect effects are combined, the positive direct impact of Democratic Party control on redistribution is more than offset by negative indirect effects. Because Democrats reduce unemployment and have such a strong equalizing effect on government conditioned pre-redistribution inequality, less redistribution is necessitated by economic conditions.

DOES POLITICS REALLY MATTER?

The implications of these results are twofold. First, most of the reduction in inequality that can be attributed to politics likely occurs via the market conditioning mechanism. Second, these results raise the possibility that reductions in pre-redistribution inequality generated by political change are offset by indirect reductions in redistribution. We must reconsider a fundamental question: Does politics really matter for distributional outcomes in the United States? To answer this question, I utilize two approaches. First, I capitalize on the fact that the overall level of post-government inequality is a perfect function of pre-redistribution inequality and redistribution. Because of this, I am able to decompose the overall effect of politics on post-government inequality by utilizing information from the models estimated in the previous section. Second, I utilize a simulation to show what the path of income inequality would have been in the absence of the Johnson administration and his Great Society initiatives.

Parsing the Effects of Politics on Distributional Outcomes

To determine the overall impact of politics on distributional outcomes, I begin by isolating the impact that changes in government conditioned market inequality and redistribution have on post-government inequality. We know that politics influences both pre-redistribution inequality and redistribution, but I want to know whether politics influences the final distribution of income that is a product of both state-conditioned market forces and explicit state redistribution.

   To plumb this question, it is important to remember that post-government inequality is, in fact, defined by pre-redistribution inequality and explicit redistribution:

$$\text{Pre}\left(1 - \frac{\text{Redistribution}}{100}\right) = \text{Post} \qquad (6.8)$$

As a starting point, we can insert the observed values for pre-redistribution inequality, redistribution, and post-government inequality from 2000 into the equation to produce the following:

$$5.645\left(1 - \frac{65.899}{100}\right) = 1.925 \qquad (6.9)$$

What is the impact of a unit increase in both Democratic control and policy liberalism? The unstandardized impact of party control on redistribution, we know from Table 6.2, is −5.76. The impact of a unit increase in policy liberalism on redistribution is 0.036. Thus, the model predicts that explicit redistribution would decrease from 65.899 (the observed amount in 2000) to 60.179. Conducting similar calculations for pre-redistribution inequality predicts a decrease from 5.645 to 4.563. Inserting these values into the post-government inequality equation produces:

$$4.563 \left(1 - \frac{60.179}{100} \right) = 1.817 \qquad\qquad (6.10)$$

We know from the results discussed earlier in the chapter that the total impact of a leftward shift in politics is a decline in pre-redistribution inequality and a simultaneous decrease in redistribution. Despite these countervailing effects of politics on inequality via the market conditioning (decreasing inequality) and redistributive (increasing inequality) mechanisms, we see here that the overall impact of a leftward shift in the macro political landscape is a reduction in post-government inequality.

There are several additional pieces of information that can be gleaned from repeating the above procedure under slightly modified circumstances. First, while I will not repeatedly go through the calculation, I have computed the effect of a policy change and a change in party control separately. The results of this calculation indicate that a one standard deviation increase in policy liberalism produces a 0.060 reduction in post-government inequality. A comparable increase in party control reduces post-government inequality by 0.051. The conclusion is that the overall impact of political power resources and macro politics is split almost evenly between policy and partisan effects.

Second, I can calculate the overall impact of the market conditioning and explicit redistribution mechanisms induced by changes in party control and public policy. It should be obvious that the entire equalizing impact of Democratic control of the presidency occurs via the market conditioning mechanism, since the total impact of Democratic control on redistribution is actually negative. But policy liberalism decreases inequality both by decreasing pre-redistribution inequality and increasing redistribution. Since both the market conditioning and explicitly redistributive impact of a leftward policy shift produce less inequality, the relative importance of these mechanisms is less clear with regard to policy liberalism. Overall, a unit-increase in policy liberalism produces a reduction in post-government inequality of o.oo6. Isolating the effects via pre-redistribution inequality (market conditioning) and redistribution shows that approximately 67 percent of the total equalizing effect occurs via market conditioning and 33 percent via redistribution. This is direct evidence that the lion's share of political influence on distributional outcomes occurs via the market conditioning mechanism as opposed to explicit redistribution. In welfare states such as the United States, then, the classic focus on redistribution results in misleading conclusions.

The final important bit of information to be gleaned from Table 6.2 is that public opinion exerts a substantial impact on distributional outcomes. The standardized impact of a liberal shift in public opinion on pre-redistribution inequality is positive and substantial when compared to other explanatory variables. As with party control and in large part attributable to indirect effects via party control, liberalism in public opinion actually reduces redistribution. Again, however, calculating the effects on post-government inequality shows that the reductions in redistribution do not cancel out the reductions in pre-redistribution inequality. So more liberal public opinion results in less inequality.

Simulating the Distributional Impact of Lyndon B. Johnson

Thus far in discussing the substantive impact of political change on distributional outcomes, I have focused on assessing the effect that arbitrary hypothetical changes in public policy and party control of the presidency would have using observed data from 2000 as a baseline. I want to move this discussion a bit closer to political reality by simulating the effect of a counter-factual in the observed data. Specifically, I use the model estimated earlier in the chapter to simulate the impact of a Republican president replacing Lyndon Johnson from 1965 to 1968 and the erasure of the Great Society programs enacted during 1965. In other words, what path would post-government inequality have taken if party control of the presidency would have diverged from its actual path for 4 years in the 1960s and a permanent conservative deviation from observed policy liberalism would have occurred since 1965?[4]

While it is not fully possible to re-run history to see what would have happened, I can use information from the estimated models to generate a prediction of post-government inequality based on the imagined scenario that LBJ was not president and his left policies not enacted. The counter-factual I propose for presidential control, then, is straightforward: replace the Democratic presidency of LBJ with a Republican. The policy counter-factual is a bit more complicated. The year 1965 marked a watershed in liberal lawmaking, with the passage of fifteen liberal laws. My counter-factual for policy liberalism is simply that 1965 would have been a "normal" year of lawmaking, meaning that the usual 2.19 major liberal laws had been passed. This means the simulation will examine a reduction of 12.81 in policy liberalism from 1965 to the present.

The first step in the simulation is to calculate predicted changes in pre-redistribution inequality that would result from the counter-factual. The second step is to simulate the predicted changes for redistribution. Finally, simulated post-government inequality is calculated from simulated pre-redistribution inequality and redistribution. One of the interesting things about this counter-factual is that it provides a detailed picture of the dynamic effects of politics on distributional outcomes. Recall that my use of error-correction models allows for the possibility that a portion of the impact of a change in an explanatory variable occurs completely during a short time-frame, such as when a change in immigration this year produces a change in pre-redistribution inequality next year. But the ECM also accounts for the possibility that a shift in an explanatory variable might have an impact that is spread out over a longer time frame, such as when it takes about 8 years to see the full impact of a change in presidential party control on redistribution. The simulation, unlike the static estimates discussed earlier, accounts for the dispersal of impact over time that occurs via the error correction component. In the static estimates,

---

[4] A shift in policymaking in any one year creates a permanent shift in policy liberalism because policy liberalism is computed by accumulating policymaking over time. Thus, a more conservative level of policymaking in a given year will automatically produce a more conservative level of policy in all years after the conservative policy shock. More details on the policy liberalism measure are in the previous chapter.

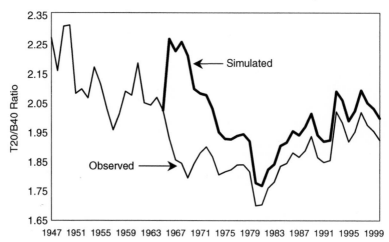

FIGURE 6.4. Actual and Simulated Post-Government Inequality without LBJ and 1965 Great Society Programs

I calculated the total impact that would eventually occur given a sustained change in the explanatory variable. This simulation allows us to see how long-term effects via error correction develop over time and how an impermanent 4-year change in party control of the presidency manifests itself over a 35-year period.

Figure 6.4 shows the observed path of post-government inequality as well as its simulated path after replacing LBJ with a Republican and eliminating the liberal policymaking of the Great Society with an average year of lawmaking. The initial impact of the counter-factual is impressive. The deviation between the simulated path of inequality and its actual path peaks at 23 percent in 1969. However, due to the dissipating effect of the temporary change in the presidency, the deviation between the counter-factual and reality declines steadily from 1969 to 1981. Whereas simulated inequality is 23 percent higher than observed inequality in 1969, this drops to a 4 percent discrepancy by the 1980s and remains at a similar level to the end of the simulation. By the end of the simulation, we are seeing only the effect of the policy shift, which was a permanent reduction in policy liberalism that persisted since 1965. While the gap between the two series is seemingly small by the end, inequality would still have been 4 percent higher in 2000 had it not been for the Great Society.

CONCLUSION

The analysis in this chapter has clearly shown that politics matters for distributional outcomes. When Democrats are in control of government and liberal policies are enacted, income inequality declines. The mechanisms that generate this outcome are somewhat unexpected. Redistribution is clearly the most explicit mechanism that government uses to reduce inequality, but its impact is less responsive to macro political change than is pre-redistribution inequality. This indicates that political dynamics have a greater impact on distributional outcomes via what I have called the market conditioning mechanism than through explicit redistribution.

Furthermore, the analysis here shows that the dynamics of inequality reverberate back into the system, affecting the redistributive impact of the state. Political change produces change in market inequality, and changes in market inequality influence redistribution. Quite interestingly, we have seen that when Democrats control the White House, pre-redistribution inequality declines to such an extent that less redistribution occurs. To the contrary, when a Republican takes over the White House redistribution increases in tandem with overall levels of post-government inequality.

Finally, we have seen direct evidence that public opinion shapes income inequality. When public opinion shifts to the left, Democrats are elected and policy moves in a liberal direction. These changes, in turn, produce reductions in inequality. Public opinion is the engine that drives the macro political system, and it is an engine that moves not just politics, but also societal outcomes. The representational linkages discovered in the macro politics model are not empty. Shifts in public opinion are actually translated into outcomes that lie at the heart of political contestation. These results suggest a variety of conclusions, which I turn to in the final chapter.

7

Distribution, Redistribution, and the Future of American Politics

The central goal of this book has been to explore the connection between politics and distributional outcomes in America. I began with a basic description of inequality in America and developed a theoretical framework for explaining distributional outcomes in which politics plays a central role. I then discussed several ways in which the state can influence distributional outcomes, categorizing these efforts into explicit redistribution and market conditioning. The next step in the argument was to discuss the nature of partisan and ideological disagreement over distribution and redistribution in American politics. I then moved to a series of analyses that examined how macro political dynamics are connected to the dynamics of inequality in America. In this concluding chapter, I synthesize the results, discuss the major conclusions of my work, and explore predictions about the future of American income inequality that grow out of my research.

HOW DOES POLITICS INFLUENCE WHO GETS WHAT?

The question of how politics influences who gets what has multiple answers. Politics influences distributional outcomes in myriad ways, even when we just focus on the macro level as I have done in this book. In this section, I explore my major conclusions by providing several answers to this question and discussing the importance of each answer.

Politics Affects Both Distribution and Redistribution

One of the first messages that we should take is that focusing on only redistribution or only inequality is insufficient if our goal is to understand distributional outcomes. In this book I have examined both distribution, the amount of economic inequality produced by the (government conditioned) market, and redistribution, how much inequality is reduced when government takes from some and gives to others. Breaking the distributional process into two stages accomplishes at least two objectives. First, it provides us with an ability to examine how "market" outcomes are influenced by political dynamics. Second, it helps to avoid misleading conclusions that come from focusing just on redistribution or money income inequality.

This second point deserves a bit more discussion. The standard dependent variable in studies of American income inequality is either family or household *money* income inequality. The problem with money income is that it only partially accounts for the redistributive impact of government. It includes benefits from cash transfer programs but does not include in-kind benefits from programs such as food stamps. Neither does it account for the impact of taxes. In other words, money income is not a very useful concept because it is neither a clear measure of market inequality nor a clear measure of post-government inequality.

My strategy was to examine the distributional process in two explicit stages, the first stage being primarily determined by market forces and the second stage being influenced primarily by government policy. The two stages combine to produce a final distribution of income, which is a combination of market and governmental forces and can be measured utilizing the posttax post-transfer income concept. Creating the measures necessary to follow this strategy is certainly much more time-consuming than simply going to the latest Census publications and recording the official level of income inequality that is defined by money income. But following this strategy opened the door to an examination of government's impact on both stages of the distributional process and allowed an analysis of how market and political forces are interconnected. Many of the results discussed throughout the book would simply be impossible without this two-stage conceptualization of the distributional process in the United States.

The Power Resources of the Lower Classes Influence Distributional Outcomes

If we want to know how politics influences who gets what in America, the results here point toward power resources theory as a fruitful framework. Despite the fact that power resources theory had its origins in the expansive welfare states of Europe, the fundamental predictions apply even in the liberal welfare state of the United States. The classic indicators of both market and political power resources have their expected impact on distributional outcomes. Decreasing levels of union membership, as an indicator of market power resources, have led to a less equal distribution of income. In the United States, however, political power resources take center stage as a predictor of distributional outcomes. Left party strength produces substantial reductions in income inequality in America.[1] This is all consistent with power resources theory. In addition, to assess power resources theory in a new way that goes beyond party control of government, I examined the ideological tone of public policy. I find that leftward shifts in public policy reduce economic inequities in the United States.

Who Gets What is Determined by, and is a Part of, the Macro Political System

The macro politics literature has tended to examine the causes of opinion change – media coverage, consumer confidence, thermostatic feedback in response to policy – as well as the consequences of opinion change – differential electoral outcomes and public policies. This book moves the causal nexus forward by asking whether the macro political dynamics that begin with the formation of public opinion and then work themselves through representational linkage into policymaking then also extend to policy outcomes – specifically the dynamics of equality between the rich and the poor. The answer I have found is a resounding yes.

That party control of government and the ideological tone of policymaking influence distributional outcomes is an important contribution and certainly extends the logic of the macro politics model to an

---

[1] This is the case despite the commonly held view that there is little difference between Democrats and Republicans in American politics. The Democrats may not be a traditional left party in the comparative sense, but differences between the American parties are translated into divergent distributional outcomes when the electoral balance of power shifts.

important societal outcome. However, that is not the end of the story. What we have seen, by analyzing distributional outcomes in two stages, is that just as policy affects the dynamics of inequality, the dynamics of inequality reverberate back into the system, having causal effects of their own. Yes, party control and policy influence market inequality, with shifts to the left decreasing inequality, but market inequality also influences redistribution. When market inequality moves higher, redistribution responds by shifting upward as well. By the same token, redistribution is influenced by political dynamics but also conditions market decisions thereby influencing the market distribution of income. In this sense, gains and losses in economic equality are squarely within the *system* of American political dynamics.

For Distributional Outcomes, Political Dynamics are Similar in Importance to Demographic and Economic Change

Macro political dynamics, of course, are not the only factors that influence distributional outcomes. However, for far too long politics has been relegated to the periphery. Economists in large part ignore the role of government in producing distributional outcomes. Sociologists have paid attention to politics, but political dynamics are still not central to their story. Here we have seen that political change fits nicely alongside both economic and demographic explanations of distributional outcomes. In fact, the evidence presented in this book points to the conclusion that politics is nearly as important in explaining income inequality as the more traditional economic and demographic explanations. To minimize the importance of politics when assessing the dynamics of inequality in the United States is pure folly. Politics is one of the few avenues through which distributional outcomes can actually be influenced. The aging of a population is a difficult thing to change. So is the globalization of an economy. These factors influence inequality, and politics is one of the few ways that anything can be done. In fact, as we have seen, politics not only directly influences distributional outcomes, but can also indirectly influence inequality in ways such as generating higher or lower levels of employment.

It's the (Market) Economy, Stupid!

Typically, when people talk about the role of politics in distributional outcomes, the conversation is about explicit redistribution. The debates in contemporary Washington that most often turn toward distributional concerns are those about tax cuts and benefit programs, even ones like the marriage penalty tax that are not inherently linked to redistributional questions. Democrats consistently criticize Republicans for wanting to cut taxes for the rich, and Republicans accuse Democrats of wanting to hand out money to the (undeserving) poor. There is no doubt that taxes and transfers decrease inequality in America. When it comes to political dynamics, however, redistribution is a relatively small part of the story. This is consistent with what we observed when asking policymakers in Washington about their distributional preferences.

According to the survey of House members reported in Chapter 3, Democrats and Republicans largely agree that redistribution should be avoided. This is why even Democrats are reticent to mention the dreaded "R" word in debates about government programs. A favorite critique of any expansion of an existing benefit program or new transfer program, in fact, is that it is "just more redistribution." Perhaps because of this general agreement, the amount of redistribution that occurs when left policies are enacted and Democrats control government is only slightly different than when more conservative policies are enacted by Republicans. The direct effect of a shift toward the left in the macro polity is only a slight increase in redistribution.

The larger part of the story is market conditioning. As we saw in Chapter 3, Democratic and Republican policymakers differ markedly in their preferences regarding the use of the state to create conditions in which economic opportunities are equalized. Democrats favor leftward shifts in policy that condition the market in a way that benefits those at the bottom, thus reducing market inequality. Policies supported by Republicans, however, have exactly the opposite effect, moving market inequality higher. When we look at the overall impact of political change on post-government inequality, we see that politics has a much greater impact via market conditioning than via explicit redistribution. It is important to note that this outcome may be unique to the United States. In many countries, there is not such general disdain for explicit redistribution, which brings redistribution more squarely into the realm of political contestation and likely makes it more responsive to macro political change and more important as a mechanism for political impact on distributional outcomes.

Market Conditioning and Explicit Redistribution are Used in Tandem to Influence Distributional Outcomes

While it is clear that market conditioning is the mechanism for equalizing distributional outcomes that is most responsive to macro political dynamics, it is equally clear that policymakers do not face a choice between either conditioning markets or explicitly redistributing income in order to achieve distributional objectives. To the contrary, at least when we focus on the direct effects of political dynamics on redistribution and market inequality, we find that these mechanisms are used in tandem. It would be incorrect to say that Democrats favor redistribution and Republicans favor market mechanisms to level the distributional playing field. The liberal policies favored by Democrats both directly reduce market inequality and directly increase redistribution. Democrats use both market mechanisms and explicit redistribution to achieve their distributional goals. The same can be said of Republicans, but the apparent distributional goals are different. When Republicans enact conservative policies, the direct effect is a reduction in redistribution and an increase in market inequality. It simply is not the case that both parties have the same objectives but simply pursue different means to the same end. Both parties utilize market conditioning and redistribution in pursuit of divergent distributional outcomes.

Equalizing Distributional Outcomes Does Not Necessarily Lead to a Bloated Traditional Welfare State

Republicans routinely charge that Democrats seek a welfare state that is out of control, redistributing income in excessive amounts and thus reducing the incentives necessary for innovation and economic growth. They are partially correct, in that the increased redistribution that is directly advocated by many Democrats does have the indirect consequence of increasing pre-redistribution inequality. What unravels this critique, however, is that the real action on distributive outcomes is in the realm of market conditioning. The empirical evidence is clear. When the direct and indirect effects of Democratic control of government are considered, they actually reduce redistribution, rather than increase it. This is because Democrats reduce pre-redistribution inequality by intervening in markets via market conditioning to such an extent that redistributive programs become less necessary. At the same time, Republicans indirectly increase redistribution by enacting policies that exacerbate pre-redistribution inequality.

In the end, the distributional outcomes produced by the parties are in line with expectations. Inequality rises when Republicans are in charge and declines under Democratic control. However, it is interesting to note that much of the equalizing impact induced by Democrats can be attributed to market conditioning mechanisms rather than explicit redistribution. These market conditioning mechanisms might also be described as mechanisms that equalize economic opportunities. The caricature of Democrats as interested in equality of outcome and Republicans as supportive of equality of opportunity seems only partially correct. Democrats primarily achieve equality of outcome through opening market opportunities to those at the bottom of the pre-redistribution income scale. Republicans, it seems, oppose such market conditioning schemes favored by Democrats and, in the process, inadvertently induce the need for more government redistribution. This is an ironic outcome to say the least.

Americans Can Modify Distributional Outcomes, If They Want To

Extending the macro politics model to distributional outcomes produced an additional important finding – public opinion influences distributional outcomes. Previous studies at the aggregate level have found that public opinion influences policymaking, and this has been interpreted as successful democratic representation. But a well-functioning democracy requires both representation and accountability. That is, the policies enacted must actually make a difference. If public opinion shifts toward the left, policy responds, but important societal outcomes that should be influenced by changing government policy do not respond, how successful would dynamic representation really be? In addition, there has been recent debate about the responsiveness of government to smaller segments of society. For example, members of Congress may be more responsive to rich constituents than to the poor (Bartels 2006, Bartels 2008) and Gilens (2006) argues that policy responds to some segments of the population more than others, but Soroka and Wlezien (2006) present evidence in favor of the idea that macro policy is remarkably responsive to all segments of the population. My analysis does not speak directly to the relative responsiveness of policy and economic outcomes to different segments of the mass public, but I can say that public opinion influences distributional outcomes in the way we would expect. When public opinion shifts toward the left, the composition of government and policies enacted by government also shift toward the left. Then, these mass-driven changes in government produce changes in the income distribution. Pre-redistribution inequality is dramatically reduced, as is the overall level of inequality. If the mass public demands less inequality, they can have it, and the reverse, of course, is also true. Regardless of one's distributional preferences, this should be encouraging news.[2]

All of the conclusions discussed above point toward an overarching finding in support of my combination of the macro politics model and power resources theory. While work in the macro politics tradition has focused on explaining the causes and consequences of public opinion with a particular emphasis on how opinion is translated into policy change, power resources theory pointed my examination of the U.S. macro political system toward a focus on distributional outcomes. Allowing these approaches, one from American politics and one from comparative politics, to inform my work produced a useful framework to study the distributional process in the United States.

By bringing these approaches together, I was not only able to gain understanding of income inequality in America, but also able to provide useful extensions both to the macro politics model and power resources theory. I extended the macro politics model beyond policymaking and found that distributional outcomes are of central importance in U.S. macro political dynamics. Income inequality is not only influenced by macro political change, but it is also apparent that distributional outcomes shape the macro political system itself. With regard to power resources theory, I found a great deal of support for its predictions even in the least-likely case of the United States. I also extended the logic of power resources theory to the realm of market conditioning, finding that government-conditioned market inequality

---

[2] Of course some historical legacies are very difficult to overcome with a mere change in preferences. Black Americans, for example, have faced many institutional hurdles to their economic advancement. My analysis only accounts for such historical legacies in a very general empirical sense. Taking account of these historical processes would require a much different analytical approach that the one employed here. Nonetheless, the importance of history should not be dismissed.

is highly responsive to changes in the actualization of lower class power resources.

The general point that can be drawn from this approach to understanding distributional outcomes in the United States is that communication and cross-fertilization between the fields of political science can be very fruitful. In fact, such cross-field theoretical development is probably most useful with regard to the largest and most important unanswered questions in our discipline. While this may be readily acknowledged by many of us in political science, we should actively look for such cross-field opportunities.

AMERICAN INEQUALITY IN THE TWENTY-FIRST CENTURY: LOOKING FORWARD

The last half of the twentieth century brought a great deal of change in inequality. After decreasing for nearly 25 years, inequality began a fairly steady march toward greater inequality during the early 1970s. What is the future of inequality in America? There are several current trends that shed some light on this question, and many political decisions will in part determine the future path of inequality in the United States.

There are a variety of trends which point to additional increases in inequality in the future. Perhaps the most important of these trends is our increasingly service-based, global economy. As service-sector jobs that are often low-paying and free of union representation become more prevalent, market inequality is likely to rise both because of declining market power resources and the logic of industrialism. Likewise, an aging population with higher proportions of retirees and elderly individuals with declining health puts upward pressure on market inequality. Finally, the current trend toward ever higher executive salaries (relative to other employees) is likely to feed an upward trend in market income inequality. Market and demographic forces will almost undoubtedly exacerbate economic inequality.

But as we have seen, market and demographic factors are only part of the equation. Furthermore, market inequality is only the first stage of the distributional process. While current trends certainly make it seem likely that inequality will maintain its currently high level or even increase further, the reaction of the state to these forces will in large part determine the overall level of inequality present after market outcomes are conditioned and government redistributes income. The path that our society will choose is yet to be determined. The questions are how we will deal with the market and demographic factors that tend to force inequality higher and whether or not government will enact new policies to reduce the gap between rich and poor.

Clearly, current economic and demographic trends are likely to exert continued upward pressure on economic inequality in the United States. If we focus on distributional outcomes as a part of the U.S. governing system, however, there is some reason to believe that income inequality will not rise and may, in fact, fall in the near term. The dynamics of the American macro political system begin with the formation of public opinion, and we have seen that shifts in public opinion eventually have distributional consequences. Current levels of Public Mood liberalism suggest that equalizing changes are on the horizon. The most recent macro public opinion data (Stimson's Mood measure in 2004) shows that public opinion is currently more liberal than it has been since just before the Great Society programs were enacted in the mid-1960s. The recent switch in party control of Congress shows that these preferences are beginning to be translated into election outcomes and will likely produce policy change in the near future.

If public opinion translates into greater Democratic strength in government and leftward shifts in public opinion, this will place downward pressure on market income inequality. We must be careful to note that this does not necessarily mean observed market inequality will fall. To the contrary, if market and demographic change places sufficient upward pressure on income inequality, liberal policies will simply slow the growth of economic inequality. I suspect, however, that liberal policy enactments will condition market outcomes sufficiently to prevent market inequality from rising, and may even produce slight reductions in inequality. The minimum wage will rise, protections for foreign workers will be added to free trade agreements, executive compensation will come under fire, and the elimination of workforce discrimination will be vigorously pursued.

At the same time, Democrats will act to protect the largest redistributive programs in the United States, most especially Social Security. Privatization of Social Security, for example, will most likely not be a serious part of the agenda if Democrats are powerful in Washington.

Proposals to expand the redistributive state will also be more likely to gain traction. The most important changes on this front are likely to come in the domain of health care. Democrats will likely try to either create new redistributive programs to help millions of Americans pay for health care, or they will create strong incentives or even requirements for employers to provide health benefits for their employees. The former strategy for expanding health coverage would be an expansion of the classic redistributive state, while proposals focused on employer provision of benefits would be an example of market conditioning. In the end, without major new redistributive programs, reduced market inequality produced by liberal policy will decrease the need for redistribution and will reduce overall levels of post-government inequality while at the same time reducing explicit redistribution.

However, if Republicans once again gain ascendancy in Washington, tax cuts and reductions in domestic spending will likely be the order of the day. Clearly, a current target of conservative policymakers is Social Security. While it is clear that present benefit levels cannot be maintained indefinitely, the most extreme ideas about privatizing the program would lead to both a reduction in redistribution and an increase in market inequality. The reasons for the reduction in redistribution are obvious. Privatizing Social Security amounts to taking a redistributive program and shifting it to the private sector. The increase in market inequality is less certain, but without major controls on how individuals might invest for their retirement, it is likely that some would make very good choices and some would make rather bad ones. Those who make good investment choices would leap far ahead of those making worse decisions (or those who are just unlucky). This is not to say that those at the bottom will not be better off in absolute terms (rather than relative terms) under a private system. I do not have an answer to that question. What seems clear, however, is that inequality would increase under such a policy shift, and it would increase via both mechanisms of government influence on distributional outcomes that were discussed in this book – market conditioning and redistribution.

The message of this book is that in the realm of distributional outcomes, America in some part controls its own destiny. We are not *simply* at the mercy of a global economy and demographic realities, though those factors certainly do matter. Through politics, distributional outcomes can be influenced dramatically. This influence is not likely to occur via policies that explicitly redistribute income, but instead can come through programs that augment the economic opportunities of the poor. The battle over distributional outcomes is an essential part of the macro political system. If the American public wants less inequality, they can affect this outcome by their preferences and their voting behavior. By the same token, if Americans want to see inequality increase as economic and demographic conditions continue to place upward pressure on economic inequality, this outcome can also be achieved. "Who gets what?" is in part determined by economic and demographic factors that are difficult if not impossible to control, but a large part of the answer to this question can be determined by the dynamics of the macro political system – and citizens are a central component in this system.

Appendix A: Congressional Questionnaire

«ID»

Thank-you for participating in this research project. Please answer each of the following questions to the best of your ability.

1) Please rank order the following outcomes from 1 to 7 with 1 being your most important priority and 7 being the least important in your thinking when developing and voting on legislation.

_____ Increasing Labor Productivity

_____ Decreasing Unemployment

_____ Increasing Economic Growth

_____ Decreasing Income Inequality

_____ Increasing International Trade

_____ Reducing Poverty

_____ Controlling Inflation

2) The following is a list of occupations. On the line next to each occupation, please write about how much (in US $) you think an average individual in each profession **SHOULD** earn during a year, regardless of the amount they actually earn.

a) Computer Programmer .... _____

b) Construction Worker .... _____

c) Janitor .... _____

d) CEO of Fortune 500 Company .... _____

e) Fast Food Employee .... _____

f) Physician .... _____

g) Plumber .... _____

h) Factory Line Employee .... _____

i) Human Resources Manager .... _____

j) Certified Financial Planner .... _____

PLEASE COMPLETE REVERSE SIDE.

(3)   The items on this page refer to the following scale, where 1 indicates strong disagreement, 7 indicates strong agreement, and the numbers 2, 3, 4, 5, and 6 represent levels of agreement between these two extremes.

Strongly Disagree   Strongly Agree

1	2	3	4	5	6	7

Circle the number that best approximates your opinion on each of the following statements:

(a)   To ensure the best economic outcomes, government must sometimes intervene in the market.

1	2	3	4	5	6	7

(b)   Society is better off when the income gap between the richest and poorest individuals is reduced.

1	2	3	4	5	6	7

(c)   It is inappropriate for government to implement programs that redistribute income from the rich to the poor.

1	2	3	4	5	6	7

(d)   Government has a responsibility to modify some market processes in order to provide equal economic opportunities to all citizens.

1	2	3	4	5	6	7

(e)   Differences in income between the richest and poorest individuals in society are necessary to ensure a strong economy.

1	2	3	4	5	6	7

(f)   Government should provide explicit benefits to the following groups:

	1	2	3	4	5	6	7
(i) Stockholders	1	2	3	4	5	6	7
(ii) The Aged	1	2	3	4	5	6	7
(iii) Small Businesses	1	2	3	4	5	6	7
(iv) The Poor	1	2	3	4	5	6	7
(v) Veterans	1	2	3	4	5	6	7
(vi) Corporate Executives	1	2	3	4	5	6	7
(vii) Children	1	2	3	4	5	6	7
(viii) Doctors	1	2	3	4	5	6	7

Please include any additional comments you might have.

Appendix B: Measuring Income Inequality over Time

The analysis focuses on three concepts related to the two stages of the distributional process – pre-redistribution inequality, post-government inequality, and explicit government redistribution. Measuring the concepts is a relatively straightforward undertaking in the static context of the year 2000. Data from the U.S. Census Bureau provides a wealth of information about income at the household level. In the 2000 data, for example, we can learn with a reasonable degree of precision how much income each household received from a wide variety of sources, such as wages, Social Security, dividends, Medicare benefits, and unemployment. There are also reasonable estimates of taxes that were paid within a household. Based on these data, the pre-redistribution income of each household can be computed by excluding income from all government sources. Post-government income can be computed for each household by including income from government sources and accounting for the amount of federal taxes paid. With household level data on pre-redistribution income and post-government income, a measure of inequality can be calculated for each income concept, and the redistributional impact of government can be calculated by finding the difference between pre-redistribution inequality and post-government inequality. Government redistribution could then be reported in absolute or proportional terms.

This procedure works quite well going back in time to the late 1970s. Prior to 1979, however, less detailed income data were collected. The further one goes back in time, the less detailed the income data become. An additional complication is the unit of analysis for which data are available. In the cross-sectional data discussed in Chapters 1 and 2, the unit of analysis was consistently the household – a group of related or unrelated individuals living in the same dwelling. The household as a unit of analysis is only available in the Census data since 1967. Prior to that time, data were collected for families and for groups of unrelated individuals. The household is the most appropriate unit of analysis because households include both families living together and unrelated individuals living together. So, the question is how to create consistent measures of the three central concepts – pre-redistribution inequality, post-government inequality, and explicit redistribution – moving back to the late 1940s.

The standard practice in previous studies of American income inequality has been to look only at inequality in family money income, which remained available after the switch in 1967 to the household as the standard unit of analysis in Census income data (Danziger and Gottschalk 1995). With regard to the unit of analysis, the standard practice is not ideal because examining families excludes unrelated individuals living together. With regard to income concept, money income does not align well with either pre-redistribution or post-government and certainly provides no options for examining the distributional impact of government taxes and transfers. Thus, I will follow a different strategy here.

The first issue is creating a series with a unit of analysis that is consistent over time and includes the largest possible proportion of the population. Ideally, there would be some way to examine households as the unit of analysis in the pre-1967 data. Unfortunately, this cannot be done. Completely excluding unrelated individuals by focusing only on families, however, is not a good option. Particularly as the proportion of unrelated individuals living under the same roof has increased over time, excluding such households from the analysis provides a distorted picture of inequality over time – a picture that includes a diminishing proportion of the total population. In order to have measures of the three central concepts before 1967 but also provide a consistent unit of analysis over time, I pursue an approach of combining available information about the money income of families and unrelated individuals. Combining information from these two units of analysis produces lower estimates of inequality than measures using the household as primary unit, but this strategy is certainly better than examining families alone. Combining information on families and unrelated individuals provides the opportunity to generate a long series with a consistent unit of analysis that does not exclude unrelated individuals.

The merging process works as follows. Since 1947, the Census Bureau has collected the data necessary to compute inequality in money income for unrelated individuals and families. While the individual-level data that are necessary to compute Gini coefficients are not useful for my purposes during the early years of income data collection, aggregate income shares for each quintile for families and unrelated individuals are regularly reported in Census Bureau publications. Using this information produces an estimate of income inequality that is not as accurate as that for households, but it provides a comparable measure during the full period of interest and allows a better estimate than using only family income.

In 1967, for example, the first quintile of families had about 5.5 percent ($26.8 billion) of aggregate family money income ($487.7 billion). The first quintile of unrelated individuals had 3 percent ($1.40 billion) of aggregate money income ($46.6 billion). When these two groups are combined, the first quintile held $28.2 billion of $534.3 billion, for an income share of 5 percent. Table B.1 shows similar data for all five income quintiles in 1967. As the table indicates, combining families and individuals does not reproduce the household data perfectly in that it consistently provides a lower estimate of inequality. However, this combination approach provides comparable money income share data going back to 1947 that is far superior to using family income alone.

TABLE B.1. *Distribution of Money Income for Families, Unrelated Individuals, and Households: 1967*

Quintile (%)	Families (%)	Unrelated Individuals (%)	Combined (%)	Households (%)
1	6	3	5	4
2	12	8	12	11
3	18	13	17	17
4	24	24	23	24
5	40	52	41	44

The second problem is creating measures of pre-redistribution inequality and post-government inequality with less and less detailed information about income sources as one moves back in time. In order to generate measures of the three central distributional outcomes of interest for my analysis, I follow a strategy that is similar to that of Smeeding (1979) and Browning and Johnson (1979). The logic of this method is illustrated in Table B.2. The money income received by each income quintile is the starting point of this method, and this distribution is reported in the first row of the table based on data from 2000. Money income, however, includes income from government cash transfers, so these must be removed before inequality in pre-redistribution income can be derived. While extremely detailed data about the distribution of cash transfer benefits is not available consistently in income data back to 1947, budgetary data that report the expenditures of federal government programs that distribute cash benefits are available.

In years that detailed income data are available (particularly after 1979), it is a straightforward matter to allocate federal cash

TABLE B.2. *A Method for Computing Income Distribution Over Time Illustrated with Data from 2000*

Income Component	Money Income Quintile ($Billions)					
	1	2	3	4	5	Total
1. Money Income	$267	$578	$925	$1395	$2903	$6077
Subtract:						
2. Cash Transfers	$270	$141	$76	$53	$47	$587
Add:						
3. Underreporting	$49	$65	$86	$111	$236	$547
Equals:						
4. Pre-Redist.	$46	$502	$935	$1453	$3092	$6037
Share	1%	8%	16%	24%	51%	
Add:						
5. Cash Transfers	$270	$141	$76	$53	$47	$587
6. In-kind Benefits	$209	$85	$53	$41	$43	$431
Subtract:						
7. Taxes	$17	$83	$215	$381	$961	$1657
Equals:						
8. Post-Gov't.	$508	$645	$849	$1166	$2221	$5398
Share	10%	12%	16%	22%	41%	

transfer outlays across the five income quintiles. Based on the detailed individual-level data, we know the proportion of total cash transfers received by each income quintile. This information combined with budget data on cash transfers in a given year can be used to determine the amount of income received by each quintile. While it may seem odd to go through this convoluted process for years in which income source specific unit-level data are available, maintaining consistency in measurement in the more recent data necessitates applying similar methods to data over the entire period of analysis.

For earlier years when detailed income data are not available, a similar logic applies, but we have less information available regarding which income quintiles received transfers. Fortunately, fiscal incidence studies have paid a great deal of attention to the distribution of government benefits across the income quintiles (Browning 1985). What we have learned from fiscal incidence studies is that the distribution of federal cash transfers across income quintiles has remained relatively steady over time. Thus, we can use what is known about the distribution of cash transfers in later years with highly detailed unit-level data to allocate cash transfers across the income quintiles in earlier years when the data are less detailed.[1] This adjustment is shown in the second row of Table B.2. One further adjustment based on known under-reporting of certain forms of income in the Census data is shown in the third row. Adjusting for under-reporting produces pre-redistribution quintile shares which are reported in the fourth row. The pre-redistribution quintile shares computed in this way are almost identical to those reported in Chapter 3, with the only discrepancy being slightly less inequality than in the household data reported earlier, which is to be expected.

The fifth, sixth, and seventh rows of the table present adjustments to pre-redistribution income that are necessary to create post-government income – cash transfers are reintroduced, the effects of in-kind benefits are added, and taxes are subtracted. As with cash transfers, consistently available budgetary data are used to determine the total government expenditures for in-kind benefits such as food stamps and Medicare.

---

[1] The proportional allocation of cash transfers among the income quintiles in years prior to 1979 are computed based on the formula computed with the detailed unit-level data available in 1979.

Since the distribution of these benefits is essentially identical for years in which unit-level in-kind benefit income data are available, these expenditures are distributed among the five income quintiles using the same formula each year, with the lowest quintiles receiving most of these expenditures. For taxes, the Internal Revenue Service has reported the total amount of revenue collected via personal tax vehicles for many years. The distribution of these taxes for each year is based on tax incidence research (Pechman and Okner 1974, Pechman 1985). Despite massive changes in tax laws, for most years the top quintile paid between 55 percent and 65 percent of these taxes and the lowest quintile paid no more than 3 percent.

The amount of post-government income received by each income quintile and the share of aggregate income this amount represents are displayed at the bottom of Table B.2. Using the methods described above, the 2000 data reported in this table are extremely close to the estimates produced by the more detailed individual-level analysis discussed in Chapter 3, again with the expected difference that household data used in Chapter 3 produce slightly higher estimates of post-government inequality than the estimate here. Most importantly, however, applying this method allows for a valid estimate of pre-redistribution inequality, post-government inequality, and explicit redistribution in every year from 1947 to 2000. The Gini coefficient cannot be computed accurately using anything less than decile income shares (I have only quintile shares), but calculating the T20/B40 ratio (ratio of the aggregate income of the top 20 percent of the income distribution to the bottom 40 percent) is possible. Using the procedures discussed above, we see that the pre-redistribution T20/B40 ratio was 5.64 and the post-government ratio was 1.93 in the year 2000 – an absolute reduction of 3.71 and a proportional reduction of 66 percent.

It is important to point out that the proportional reduction in inequality is higher in my data than in the LIS data utilized in cross-national research due to the fact that cross-national studies rely primarily on the Gini coefficient. The Gini coefficient is less sensitive to changes in distribution at the extremes of the income distribution than the T20/B40 ratio. The T20/B40 ratio, in fact, focuses exclusively on changes in distribution between the top and the bottom. So, if inequality in the middle of the income distribution (inequality among those in the middle two or three quintiles) remains fairly constant and redistribution occurs primarily between the top and bottom of the distribution, the T20/B40 ratio will be much more sensitive to such redistribution than the Gini. Given the liberal welfare state regime present in the United States, which emphasizes means-tested and targeted welfare state programs, it is fully expected that my measure of inequality would produce higher estimates of redistribution than a measure of redistribution based on changes in the Gini coefficient. Movement over time in the two types of measures, however, would be similar.

Bibliography

Alesina, Alberto and Edward Glaeser. 2006. *Fighting Poverty in the US and Europe: A World of Difference.* New York: Oxford University Press.

Alesina, Alberto and Howard Rosenthal. 1995. *Partisan Politics, Divided Government, and the Economy.* New York: Cambridge University Press.

Banerjee, Anindya. 1986. "Exploring Equilibrium Relationships in Econometrics through Static Models: Some Monte Carlo Evidence." *Oxford Bulletin of Economics and Statistics* 48(3): 253–277.

Banerjee, Anindya, Juan Dolabo, John Galbraith and David F. Hendry. 1993. *Co-integration, Error Correction, and the Econometric Analysis of Non-Stationary Data.* New York: Oxford University Press.

Bartels, Larry M. 2006. "Is the Water Rising? Reflections on Inequality and American Democracy." *PS: Political Science and Politics* 39(1): 39–42.

Bartels, Larry M. 2008. *Unequal Democracy: The Political Economy of a New Guilded Age.* Princeton: Princeton University Press.

Beach, Charles M. and Frederick S. Balfour. 1983. "Estimated Payroll Tax Incidence and Aggregate Demand for Labour in the United Kingdom." *Economica* 50(197): 35–48.

Bradley, David, Evelyne Huber, Stephanie Moller, François Nielsen and John Stephens. 2003. "Distribution and Redistribution in Post-Industrial Democracies." *World Politics* 55(2): 193–228.

Brandolini, Andrea and Timothy Smeeding. 2006. "Patterns of Economic Inequality in Western Democracies: Some Facts on Levels and Trends." *PS: Political Science and Politics* 39(1): 21–26.

Browning, Edgar K. 1985. "Tax Incidence, Indirect Taxes, and Transfers." *National Tax Journal* 38(4): 525–533.

Browning, Edgar K. 2002. "The Case Against Income Redistribution." *Public Finance Review* 30(6): 509–530.

Browning, Edgar K. and William R. Johnson. 1979. *The Distribution of the Tax Burden.* Washington: American Enterprise Institute for Public Policy Research.

Campbell, Angus, Philip E. Converse, Warren E. Miller and Donald E. Stokes. 1960. *The American Voter.* New York: Wiley.

Dahl, Robert A. 1967. *Pluralist Democracy in the United States.* Chicago: Rand McNally.

Danziger, Sheldon and Peter Gottschalk. 1995. *America Unequal.* New York: Russell Sage Foundation.

Danziger, Sheldon, Robert Haveman and Robert Plotnick. 1981. "How Income Transfers Affect Work, Savings, and the Income Distribution." *Journal of Economic Literature* 19(3): 975–1028.

Davidson, James E. H., David F. Hendry, F. Srba and S. Yeo. 1978. "Econometric Modelling of the Aggregate Time-Series Relationship between Consumers' Expenditure and Income in the United Kingdom." *Economic Journal* 88(352): 661–692.

De Boef, Suzanna. 2001. "Modeling Equilibrium Relationships: Error Correction Models with Strongly Autoregressive Data." *Political Analysis* 9(1): 78–94.

De Boef, Suzanna and Jim Granato. 1999. "Testing for Cointegrating Relationships with Near-Integrated Data." *Political Analysis* 8(1): 99–117.

De Boef, Suzanna and Luke Keele. 2008. "Taking Time Seriously." *American Journal of Political Science* 52(1): 184–200.

Engle, Robert F. and Clive W. J. Granger. 1987. "Co-integration and Error Correction: Representation, Estimation, and Testing." *Econometrica* 55(2): 251–276.

Enns, Peter K. and Paul M. Kellstedt. 2008. "Policy Mood and Political Sophistication: Why Everybody Moves Mood." *British Journal of Political Science* 38: 433–454.

Erikson, Robert S., Michael. MacKuen and James A. Stimson. 2002. *The Macro Polity.* New York: Cambridge University Press.

Esenwein, Gregg A. 2001. The Federal Income Tax and the Treatment of Married Couples: Background and Analysis. Technical Report RL30800 Congressional Research Service.

Esping-Andersen, Gøsta. 1990. *The Three Worlds of Welfare Capitalism.* Princeton, N.J.: Princeton University Press.

Euromonitor. 2002. *International Marketing Data and Statistics 2002, 26th ed.* Chicago: Euromonitor International.

Gilens, Martin. 2006. "Inequality and Democratic Responsiveness." Paper presented at the annual meeting of the American Political Science Association, Philadelphia, PA, Aug. 31–Sept. 3.

Gottschalk, Peter and Timothy M. Smeeding. 1997. "Cross National Comparisons of Earnings and Income Inequality." *Journal of Economic Literature* 35(2): 633–687.

Harris, Fredrick C., Valeria Sinclair-Chapman and Brian D. McKenzie. 2004. *Countervailing Forces in African-American Civic Activism, 1973–1994.* New York: Cambridge University Press.

Heclo, Hugh. 1974. *Modern Social Politics in Britain and Sweden.* New Haven, CT: Yale University Press.

Hibbs, Douglas. 1987. *The American Political Economy: Macroeconomics and Electoral Politics.* New York: Cambridge University Press.

Hibbs, Douglas A., Jr. and Christopher Dennis. 1988. "Income Distribution in the United States." *American Political Science Review* 2(2): 467–489.

Hicks, Alexander and Duane H. Swank. 1984. "Governmental Redistribution in Rich Capitalist Democracies." *Policy Studies Journal* 13(2): 265–287.

Hicks, Alexander and Duane H. Swank. 1992. "Politics, Institutions, and Welfare Spending in Industrialized Democracies, 1960–1982." *American Political Science Review* 86(3): 658–674.

Hicks, Alexander and Joya Misra. 1993. "Political Resources and the Growth of Welfare in Affluent Capitalist Democracies, 1960–1982." *American Journal of Sociology* 99(3): 668–710.

Hicks, Alexander M. 1999. *Social Democracy and Welfare Capitalism: A Century of Income Security Politics.* Social democracy and welfare capitalism Ithaca, N.Y.: Cornell University Press.

Holmlund, Bertil. 1983. "Payroll Taxes and Wage Inflation: The Swedish Experience." *Scandinavian Journal of Economics* 85(1): 1–15.

Howard, Christopher. 1999. *The Hidden Welfare State: Tax Expenditures and Social Policy in the United States.* Princeton, NJ: Princeton University Press.

Huber, Evelyne, Charles Ragin and John D. Stephens. 1993. "Social Democracy, Christian Democracy, Constitutional Structure and the Welfare State." *American Journal of Sociology* 99(3): 711–749.

Huber, Evelyne and John D. Stephens. 2001. *Development and Crisis of the Welfare State: Parties and Policies in Global Markets.* Chicago: The University of Chicago Press.

Iversen, Torben. 2005. *Capitalism, Democracy, and Welfare.* New York: Cambridge University Press.

Jacobs, Lawrence and Jheda Skocpal. 2005. *Inequality and American Democracy: What we Know and What we Need to Learn.* New York: Russell Sage Foundation.

Johnston, David Cay. 2007. *Free Lunch: How the Wealthiest Americans Enrich Themselves at Government Expense (and Stick You with the Bill).* New York: Portfolio.

Keister, Lisa A. 2000. *Weath in America: Trends in Wealth Inequality.* New York: Cambridge University Press.

Kellstedt, Paul, Gregory E. McAvoy and James A. Stimson. 1996. "Dynamic Analysis with Latent Constructs." *Political Analysis* 5(1): 113–150.

Kelly, Nathan J. 2004. "Does Politics Really Matter? Policy and Government's Equalizing Influence in the United States." *American Politics Research* 32(3): 264–284.

Kelly, Nathan J. 2005. "Political Choice, Public Policy, and Distributional Outcomes." *American Journal of Political Science* 49(4): 865–880.

Korpi, Walter. 1978. *The Working Class in Welfare Capitalism: Work, Unions, and Politics in Sweden.* London: Routledge and Kegan Paul.

Korpi, Walter. 1983. *The Democratic Class Struggle.* London: Routledge and Kegan Paul.

Korpi, Walter. 1985. "Power Resources Approach vs. Action and Conflict: On Causal and Intentional Explanations in the Study of Power." *Sociological Theory* 3(2): 31–45.

Korpi, Walter. 1989. "Power, Politics, and State Autonomy in the Development of Social Citizenship: Social Rights during Sickness in Eighteen OECD Countries since 1930." *American Sociological Review* 54(3): 309–329.

Lipset, Seymour Martin and Gary Marks. 2000. *It Didn't Happen Here: Why Socialism Failed in the United States.* New York: Norton.

Lockhart, Charles. 1991. "American Exceptionalism and Social Security: Complementary Cultural and Structural Contributions to Social Program Development." *Review of Politics* 53(3): 510–529.

Mayhew, David R. 2005. *Divided We Govern: Party Control, Lawmaking and Investigations, 1946–2002.* 2nd ed. New Haven: Yale University Press.

McCarty, Nolan, Keith Poole and Howard Rosenthal. 2006. *Polarized America: The Dance of Ideology and Unequal Riches.* Cambridge: MIT Press.

McGuire, Kevin T. and James A. Stimson. 2004. "The Least Dangerous Branch Revisited: New Evidence on Supreme Court Responsiveness to Public Preferences." *Journal of Politics* 66(4): 1018–1035.

Meltzer, Alan H. and Scott F. Richard. 1981. "A Rational Theory of the Size of Government." *Journal of Political Economy* 89(4): 914–927.

Moffitt, Robert. 1992. "Incentive Effects of the U.S. Welfare System: A Review." *Journal of Economic Literature* 30(1): 1–61.

Myles, John. 1984. *Old Age and the Welfare State: The Political Economy of Public Pensions.* Boston: Little, Brown.

Orloff, Ann Shola. 1996. "Gender and the Social Rights of Citizenship: The Comparative Analysis of Gender Relations and Welfare States." *American Sociological Review* 58(3): 303–328.

Page, Benjamin I. and James Roy Simmons. 2000. *What Government Can Do: Dealing with Poverty and Inequality.* Chicago: University of Chicago Press.

Page, Benjamin I. and Robert Y. Shapiro. 1992. *The Rational Public: Fifty Years of Trends in Americans' Policy Preferences.* Chicago: University of Chicago Press.

Pampel, Fred C. and John B. Williamson. 1988. "Welfare Spending in Advanced Industrial Democracies, 1950–1980." *American Journal of Sociology* 50(6): 1424–1456.

Pechman, Joseph A. 1985. *Who Paid the Taxes, 1966–85?* Washington, D.C.: Brookings Institution.

Pechman, Joseph A. and Benjamin A. Okner. 1974. *Who Bears the Tax Burden?* Washington: Brookings Institution.

Peppard, Donald M., Jr. and Douglas B. Roberts. 1977. *Net Fiscal Incidence in Michigan: Who Pays and Who Benefits?* Lansing, MI: Michigan State University.

Plotnick, Robert D., Eugene Smolensky, Eirick Evenhouse and Siobhan Reilly. 2000. The Twentieth-Century Record of Inequality and Poverty in the United States. In *The Cambridge Economic History of the United States*, ed. Stanley L. Engerman and Robert E. Gallman. Vol. 3, New York: Cambridge University Press.

Pontusson, Jonas and Lane Kenworthy. 2005. "Rising Inequality and the Politics of Redistribution in Affluent Countries." *Perspectives on Politics* 3(3): 449–471.

Quadagno, Jill. 1988. *The Transformation of Old Age Security: Class and Politics in the American Welfare State.* Chicago: University of Chicago Press.

Sawyer, Malcom. 1976. Income Distribution and Poverty in OECD Countries. Technical Report 0474-5574 Organisation for Economic Co-operation and Development.

Skocpol, Theda. 1979. *States and Social Revolutions: A Comparative Analysis of France, Russia, and China.* New York: Cambridge University Press.

Skocpol, Theda. 1992. *Protecting Soldiers and Mothers: The Political Origins of Social Policy in the United States.* Cambridge, MA: Harvard University Press.

Skocpol, Theda and Edwin Amenta. 1986. "States and Social Policies." *Annual Review of Sociology* 12: 131–157.

Smeeding, Timothy M. 1979. "On the Distribution of Net Income: Comment." *Southern Economic Journal* 45(3): 932–944.

Soroka, Stewart N. and Christopher Wlezien. 2006. "Heterogeneity and Homogeneity in Opinion-Policy Dynamics." Paper presented at the annual meeting of The American Political Science Association, Philadelphia, PA, Aug. 31–Sept. 3.

Stenberg, Carl W. and David B. Walker. 1977. "The Block Grant: Lessons from Two Early Experiments." *Publius* 7(2): 31–60.

Stephens, John D. 1979. *The Transition from Capitalism to Socialism.* London: Macmillan.

Stimson, James A. 1999. *Public Opinion in America: Moods, Cycles, and Swings.* 2nd ed. Boulder, CO: Westview Press.

Stimson, James A., Michael B. MacKuen and Robert S. Erikson. 1995. "Dynamic Representation." *American Political Science Review* 89(3): 543–565.

Stonecash, Jeffrey M., Mark D. Brewer and Mack D. Mariani. 2002. *Diverging Parties: Social Change, Realignment, and Party Polarization.* Boulder: Westview Press.

Swank, Duane. 2002. *Global Capital, Political Institutions, and Policy Change in Developed Welfare States.* New York: Cambridge University Press.

Truman, David. 1951. *The Governmental Process.* New York: Alfred A. Knopf.

Van Arnhem, J. Corina M. and Guert J. Schotsman. 1982. Do Parties Affect the Distribution of Incomes? The Case of Advanced Capitalist Democracies. In *The Impact of Parties*, ed. Francis G. Castles. Beverly Hills, CA: Sage Publications.

Verba, Sidney and Gary R. Orren. 1985. *Equality in America: The View From the Top.* Cambridge, MA: Harvard University Press.

Vroman, Wayne. 1974. "Employer Payroll Taxes and Money Wage Behaviour." *Applied Economics* 6(3): 189–204.

Wallerstein, Michael. 1999. "Wage-Setting Institutions and Pay Inequality in Advanced Industrial Societies." *American Journal of Political Science* 43(3): 649–680.

Weissburg, Robert. 2006. "Politicized Pseudo Science." *PS: Political Science and Politics* 39(1): 33–42.

Weitenberg, Johannes. 1969. "The Incidence of Social Security Taxes." *Public Finance* 24(2): 193–208.

Wilensky, Harold. 1975. *The Welfare State and Equality.* Berkeley: University of California Press.

Wlezien, Christopher. 1995. "The Public as Thermostat: Dynamics of Preferences for Spending." *American Journal of Political Science* 39(4): 981–1000.

Index

Breinigsville, PA USA
27 December 2010
252111BV00005B/4/P